THE
HIDDEN
FIRES

'You have to be brave to meddle with a beloved classic such as Nan Shepherd's *The Living Mountain*. Only rarely does one read a book whose quality of distinction is immediately apparent from the first page; Merryn Glover's *The Hidden Fires* is not just brave, it is remarkable. Her writing comes at you out of the rock; it recalls some splendid cave painting, telling as much of man as of beast and leaving us in awe of each.'
SIR JOHN LISTER-KAYE, FRSGS, OBE

'Merryn Glover's journey with Nan Shepherd in *The Hidden Fires* is one we delight to undertake with them. Utterly reliable, sturdy companions they prove to be for such a dazzling adventure into mountain, place and time. Redolent with the presence of Nan Shepherd, this book will captivate lovers of *The Living Mountain*, bringing to the physical, philosophical and literary landscapes Glover describes, both a sense of welcome familiarity and a set of new and joyous insights.'
ESTHER WOOLFSON

'*The Hidden Fires* is a book about homecoming and homemaking, of noticing and belonging. It is a joyous celebration of the process of finding yourself.'
KERRI ANDREWS

THE
HIDDEN
FIRES

A CAIRNGORMS JOURNEY
WITH NAN SHEPHERD

MERRYN GLOVER

Polygon

First published in hardback in Great Britain in 2023
by Polygon, an imprint of Birlinn Ltd

Birlinn Ltd
West Newington House
10 Newington Road
Edinburgh
EH9 1QS

9 8 7 6 5 4 3 2 1

www.polygonbooks.co.uk

ISBN 978 1 84697 575 2
ebook isbn 978 1 78885 517 4

British Library Cataloguing-in-Publication Data
A catalogue record for this book is available on
request from the British Library.

The publisher gratefully acknowledges investment from
Creative Scotland towards the publication of this book.

Typeset in Sabon LT Pro by The Foundry, Edinburgh
Printed and bound in Great Britain by Clays Ltd, Elcograf S.p.A.

For Alistair
the perfect hill companion

CONTENTS

BEGINNING

I set out on my journey in pure love.

She is old now. At eighty-four, she begins to feel something in her bones, to clear and tidy her things, to see a long way. Her thick hair is caught back in the familiar bun, iron grey and wavy except where it turns to a pure white around her face, ruddy with life, lined and loose as a beloved map. Strong, knotted hands open a forgotten drawer, fingers move papers, fall on a typed manuscript. She takes it to a garden chair above the river and reads. By the end, the light has changed, and all colour gathered to the western hills. Beyond, lies the mountain.

* * *

It was 1977 and Nan Shepherd was not finished. For the first time in years, she took out a fresh sheet of paper. 'Thirty years in the life of a mountain is nothing – the flicker of an eyelid.' So began her foreword to *The Living Mountain*, her slim but boundless book about the Cairngorms range of Scotland. That was the length of time between her first writing the text and publishing it, and, along with recording the changes in that period, she affirmed the enduring validity of her original account. Another forty-five years have passed since then; another mere blink for the massif, another cycle of change and, now, another woman charting its story.

In 2019, I was writer-in-residence for the Cairngorms National Park, which allowed me to explore the richness of the territory – both in movement and words. During that time, I found myself returning frequently to Shepherd's work. Just like the mountains at its heart, her book continues to offer new discoveries, new ways of walking, writing and wondering, new understandings of what it means to be. *The Living Mountain* is famously difficult to classify, defying genre at its time and ever since. It is mountain literature, but not about mountaineering; it is an account of walking, but without routes; it is a field guide, but spurns taxonomy; it offers portraits of people, but glories in solitude; it is politically aware, but resists manifesto; it is philosophy, but without argument. It is what we now call nature writing, though is as much about the nature of life as the life of nature. A deeply personal account of one woman's long 'traffic of love' with one mountain range, it has become a universal testament to the journey into meaning.

The Hidden Fires is an account of my pilgrimage deeper into the Cairngorms and my own sense of being, with Nan Shepherd as invisible friend: walking guide, writing tutor and fellow wonderer. I have followed in her footsteps and, like her, have not confined specific locations to specific chapters, but allowed the narrative to wander across the range and the ideas, in the same all-embracing spirit. After this opening, the twelve chapter titles are hers, but in a different order, as befits my different journey, though we converge on the last one. Throughout, I have sought to inhabit her experience – as her text invites us to do – but rather than as an actor playing out a script, I have drawn from her words to animate my own story on the great stage of the Cairngorms, discovering our intersections and divergences, our places of one mind and our points of departure. I think it would have pleased her to know that she became for me 'the perfect hill companion'. Such a person, she wrote, 'is the one whose identity is for the time being merged in that of the mountains, as you feel your own to be'. Writing this book felt like a quiet, expansive conversation across time with her, a very different woman, about a place that has shaped us both.

Her tie to this place was a world apart from mine. Nan Shepherd was a born and bred Scot who lived in the same house in a village just west of Aberdeen until her final months in a nursing home. 'I've had the same bedroom all my life!' she cheerfully announced to an interviewer on a tour of her home when she was elderly. A significant aspect of all her writing – a body of work that includes fiction and poetry – is how grounded it is in her context and how profoundly she understood it, both in landscape and culture. Her three modernist novels, published in the late 1920s and early 1930s, were all set in rural North East communities, employing the local Scots dialect in ways that were progressive at the time, and her poetry collection, *In the Cairngorms*, was, true to title, predominantly about these mountains. Finally, *The Living Mountain*, her last publication and only major non-fiction work, bears powerful witness to the breadth of her knowledge about the area, from geology and climate to flora, fauna and people.

Along with her rootedness, one of the many remarkable things about Shepherd is her lack of narrowness. She travelled with keen curiosity to South Africa and several countries in Europe. More than that, her awareness travelled around the globe and over time in her voracious reading, her prolific correspondence and her enquiring mind. Though anchored in one place, she had wide experience and a broad vision. The two dimensions shaped each other. 'Islands are united by the bottom of the sea,' she wrote in the epigraph to *In the Cairngorms.* I have the sense that I could have talked with her about almost anything and she would have invariably been interested and probably know more than me, but never show it off. She was not the showing-off type.

I began this book in March 2020 at the beginning of the Covid lockdown. In the early months of the virus, it was often said that we had not experienced a challenge on this scale since the Second World War. Poignant then, to know that is exactly when Shepherd did her own writing about the Cairngorms. 'In that disturbed and uncertain world,' she wrote, 'it was my secret place of ease.' I know exactly what she means, except there were key differences. Even though it will take a long time to measure the final cost of the pandemic – in loss of life, economic recession and widespread distress – it remains an entirely different beast to six years of global violence and all that followed. The origins of the virus and our response to it are both fraught with human failing, but they do not arise from the urge to dominate or exterminate other people. I believe that what Shepherd and her contemporaries lived through, in two world wars, must have been more destructive to hope and a sense of humanity, so I do not pretend to place our experiences on a par, but simply to reflect on how nature meets us in a time of crisis. Equally, the irony is not lost on me that the virus is a manifestation of nature, in the same way as the anopheles mosquito and cancer. One of our existential challenges is the fact that nature is not always beautiful or benign, and our relationship with it is frequently marked by struggle. Another challenge is to live the truth that we, too, are of nature and not separate from it.

There is a further significant difference between Shepherd's experience and mine. Even though it was war, she was able to take to the hills, but as I wrote the first pages, we had been in lockdown for a fortnight and asked not to go up mountains. It was counter-intuitive, especially for those of us who, like Shepherd, seek these places for restoration. But the Mountain Rescue and emergency services could not use resources helping people lost and injured up hills when there was a medical emergency across the country, nor place themselves at risk of close contact. That was understandable and necessary. It was also extremely tough on people in cities. The whole pandemic was hardest on those in urban areas and, particularly, as always, on the poor.

While Nan Shepherd lived on the south-eastern side of the Cairngorms with the River Dee flowing near her house, I am over the mountains to the north-west, on the banks of the Spey. My lockdown exercise trips took me up a small hill, into forest and beside the river and loch. Although I longed for the chance to get into the higher hills again, I learned how much there was yet to discover on my home ground and along familiar trails, if only I took long enough to notice.

Walking through the pine woods just five minutes from my house, I knelt down for the first time to look closely at the moss, then couldn't resist sinking my fingers into its soft pile. As a child, Shepherd lay down on her stomach beside her father, exploring together the entwined strands of stagmoss, or 'toadstails', as they called them. 'Though I did not know it then,' she wrote, 'I was learning my way in, through my own fingers, to the secret of growth.' The moss that I explored, spread in pale green heaps around the foot of the trees, was also made up of hundreds of feathery strands, each one delicate and leafed, together forming a soft pillow that can be a water-logged mass after rain or, like that day, dry and downy. It was unusually warm for April and the sun bright, so I flopped back on it and looked up.

Shepherd was intensely interested in perspective and what happens to our experience of landscape when we physically change how we see it. 'By so simple a matter . . . as altering the position of one's head, a different kind of world may be made to appear.' Suddenly, in the forest a stone's throw from my home, I had entered a different world. The tall, slender trunks of the Scots pines were like columns of an ancient palace, reaching up to an azure canopy. But it was a living palace, swaying quietly, each trunk circling above its still roots as the branches touched and brushed one another, whispering. High up in the tiers of green, invisible birds were piping in high notes. Higher still, a waning moon floated like a watermark against the blue, only half there, dreaming of night.

'It will take a long time to get to the end of a world that behaves like this if I do no more than turn round on my side or my back,' said Shepherd. Like her, I'm learning that the slower I go and the longer I take over a small patch of land, the more it opens itself to me. But the more it exposes my own ignorance, too. I did not know the names of those birds in the pine forest, or the kind of moss I rested on. And while I did not need to know their names to enjoy them, now having stopped to notice them properly, having experienced them with my full attention and discovered the pleasure of their existence, I found a yearning to know them better. French philosopher Simone Weil wrote that 'attention is the rarest and purest form of generosity'. It means we give of ourselves entirely to the person or object of our focus, and, in the observing, curiosity grows. Who are you, birds? What are you singing about? Are you always here or, like me, a migrant?

Unlike Shepherd, who knew this place so deeply, I am a newcomer. Born in Kathmandu, I had a nomadic upbringing across Nepal, India, Pakistan and Australia, the country of my first passport. My father counted sixty moves before I was nineteen, and quite apart from the buildings, we moved through strikingly different environments. Much of my childhood was in the Himalayan foothills of Nepal, with their high altitudes, forests, villages and terraced fields. It instilled my love of mountains from the beginning. Stays in India included the hill station at 7,000 feet in Uttarakhand where I went to school, the central plains of Maharashtra and the crowded, colourful cities of Visakhapatnam, Delhi, Lucknow, Kolkata and Amritsar. In Pakistan, we lived in Sindh province, which encompasses both the fertile Indus river valley and the dust storms and blistering temperatures of the Thar desert. Even our furloughs in Australia were itinerant, traversing from coastal areas to the hinterland, big cities to bush, Victoria's Antarctic weather fronts to Queensland's tropics.

As a missionary family, there was never money to spare, yet the experience of all these environments was rich beyond measure and I never underestimate that privilege. At the same time, it means I do not know any one place with the expertise of a life-long dweller. I have always communed with the natural world – like lying down in the those pine woods – but my response was a simple, sensory enjoyment rather than the naturalist's drive to identify and record. It is only in recent years that delight has deepened into a desire for greater knowledge, especially of the place where I now live – the Cairngorms – and especially since discovering *The Living Mountain*.

Though the book is today hailed as a masterpiece of mountain literature, Shepherd was not considered a 'mountaineer', certainly not by herself. This is perhaps because by the time the book was published, she was eighty-four and had never gained recognition in the mountaineering community. It also reflects the distinction for many that the term 'mountaineer' is reserved for those requiring ropes, while everyone else is a 'walker'. I doubt any of that mattered to her. Once over the initial draw of the summits, she did not go to the Cairngorms for sport or to prove athletic prowess, but to enjoy being in them. 'The mountain gives itself most completely when I have no destination, when I reach nowhere in particular, but have gone out merely to be with the mountain as one visits a friend, with no intention but to be with him.' She'd hated sports at school, which at her time was called 'drill' and consisted mainly of marching and exercises with clubs that had distinctly military overtones. This was deliberate, the government having decided that British losses in the Boer wars were partly down to inadequate fitness, thus tasking schools with raising tougher soldiers.

As for me, I enjoyed school sport, particularly running, which I still do, but was never good with a ball and am definitely an 'also-ran'. And I have similar feelings to Shepherd about heading into the hills. Though 'Munro bagging' – setting out to climb all of Scotland's mountains over 3,000 feet – is a perfectly worthy pursuit, the box-ticking doesn't interest me, nor am I fit enough for the races that charge across this landscape. I don't go climbing with ropes and am, at best, wobbly on skis.

In Shepherd, then, I have found a kindred spirit – a bookish, mid-life woman of no exceptional skills, who simply loves to be in mountains. We're not a rare breed. I find it heartening how many people love both literature and wilderness, the interior, book-lined shelter of libraries and the wide-open landscapes of the hills. Shepherd describes, as a child, looking at the Cairngorms from the neighbouring Monadhliath hills with longing. 'Climbing Cairngorms was then for me a legendary task, which heroes, not men, accomplished. Certainly not children.' But as she walks into them in adulthood, and grows more and more familiar, she ends up so at home that she can fall asleep on their wide flanks with nothing but sky for a tent. Though I have come to the Cairngorms from a very different background and bring a different perspective, like her I am not a mountaineer but a mountain *stravaiger*, a great old Scots word for someone who 'wanders about'.

When not wandering the Cairngorms, Shepherd's life was steeped in literature. Having studied it at the University of Aberdeen, she taught it for all her professional life at the Aberdeen School of Education, training teachers. She loved her work and told friends she would never give up her job, even in the brief window when her writing was successful. It is now widely accepted that she did not receive the sustained recognition she deserved for her novels. Though on publication they won glowing reviews, comparisons with Virginia Woolf and a place at the table of the Scottish literary renaissance, her books gradually faded from view. This is perhaps partly because she was a woman – most of the authors still celebrated from her generation are men – and partly because she was overshadowed and scorned by Lewis Grassic Gibbon, whose three-part epic *A Scots Quair*, also set in rural Aberdeenshire, dominated the scene and continues to attract international acclaim. Certainly, Shepherd did nothing to promote herself and was uncomfortable with rave reviews. 'Don't you loathe having your work over-praised?' she wrote to author friend Neil Gunn. Most of us can't imagine such a problem.

I wonder what she would make of the demands on today's writers to maintain websites, active social media accounts and a high-ranking online platform, under constant pressure to keep churning out books at speed and get attention in an increasingly crowded and clamorous market. I admire her authenticity. If she had nothing to say, she was silent; if nothing more to write, she stopped. 'I've gone dumb,' she wrote to Gunn in 1931. 'One reaches (or I do) these dumb places in life. I suppose there's nothing for it but to go on living. Speech may come. Or it may not. And if it doesn't I suppose one has just to be content to be dumb. At least not shout for the mere sake of making a noise.' Hurrah for Nan Shepherd. And hurrah that she went on living in dumbness, for it is only out of such quiet that a work like *The Living Mountain* could ever have been written.

I also admire her unflagging generosity to others. Even when her own books slipped out of print and prominence, she maintained a lively correspondence with her many writer friends and continued to review contemporary work with insight and rigour. She championed Scottish literature in particular by bringing more of it into the curriculum of her teachers' college (previously focused on the English canon) and by supporting Scottish literary organisations, publications and authors. She was a founding member of the Saltire Society and a defender of Hugh MacDiarmid's poetry and his controversial use of Scots. Meanwhile, her own masterpiece about the Cairngorms languished in a drawer. On its completion in 1945 only Neil Gunn read it, and though he insisted on its worth, he warned it would be difficult to sell: immediately post-war, publishers were struggling and risk-averse. He suggested lengthening, serialisation and illustrations, none of which Shepherd pursued. She sent one query letter to his recommended publisher, but when they declined to see the manuscript, she put it away. How characteristic of her not to keep peddling her wares round the marketplace, but how suggestive, also, that perhaps she knew the time wasn't right. As Neil Gunn wrote to her, '[T]he world doesn't want the well-water. It doesn't know that it needs it.'

Thirty years later, the world had changed out of all recognition. The Vietnam war, the social revolutions of the sixties, the emerging environmental movement and the hippy trail to Asia all fostered a greater openness to the philosophical ideas and contemplation of nature explored in

The Living Mountain. Shepherd makes no reference to any of these in her 1977 foreword, focusing solely on the changes to the Cairngorms themselves, and by way of explanation for her decision to publish at last, simply that 'the tale of my traffic with a mountain is as valid today as it was then'. Whether the world was ready or not, she clearly was. Perhaps she was goaded by an interview with a journalist the previous year who published the article under the headline 'Writer of genius gave up'. Perhaps she was persuaded by the handful of people who had, by then, read the manuscript and insisted she must get it into print. Whatever it was, she chose not to undergo further offers and rejections through traditional publishers. She was old and maybe felt she simply didn't have the time. I wonder, also, whether she decided she was done with all those gatekeepers and no longer prepared to wait for their judgements. There is a sense, for me, of a woman late in life who recognised both the value of her work and the time to act. Thankfully for posterity, it was a last-minute triumph of self-belief over her more customary self-deprecation. She did choose to include illustrations, after all, and paid for an initial print-run of 3,000 copies through Aberdeen University Press, who were only printers at the time. Effectively, she self-published it. That's usually a dirty word in traditional publishing circles, associated with vanity, delusion and obvious failure to produce writing of worth. Shepherd clearly knew better. But that still didn't make her a good saleswoman, of her own work, at any rate. With responsibility for all marketing and distribution, she gave away countless copies but only sold a few hundred, leaving most of them sitting in boxes.

It took another thirty years for the book and her writing to finally gain rightful place, partly through the championing of academics like Aileen Christianson, Roderick Watson, Alison Lumsden and Robert Macfarlane – and an ever-growing number. By now, it has sold hundreds of thousands of copies worldwide, been translated into at least sixteen languages and spawned countless works in response from dance, music, art, photography, a literary prize and further writing, including mine. Who knows what she would make of it all, in particular how she features on the Scottish five-pound note. It is a striking picture showing the quiet strength and intelligence in her face, but in long plaits and a jewelled headband that make her look like a neo-pagan about to invoke the moon goddess. That is not Nan Shepherd. In reality, the photo captures a playful moment during the shoot when the young Nan quickly improvised her accessory with photographic tape and a brooch. She inscribed the picture, 'In the days of my Norse Princess Incarnation.' Sounds like she was just dressing up and having a laugh. That is the Nan Shepherd I recognise. She had a keen sense of humour and a joyous energy and was far too down to earth to indulge fantasy versions of herself.

One of the quotes that accompanies the image is similarly deceptive. 'It's a grand thing to get leave to live,' it says. These words are also on Shepherd's flagstone in the Makars' Court in Edinburgh. They are actually spoken by the character Geordie Ironside in her first novel, *The Quarry Wood*, and come at the moment he kills a chicken by wringing its neck. It's an act Shepherd herself performed many times. As a person and a writer, she was unsentimental and both celebrated life and wryly acknowledged its ironies. The second quote is from *The Living Mountain*: 'But the struggle between frost and the force in running water is not quickly over. The battle fluctuates, and at the point of fluctuation between the motion in water and the immobility of frost, strange and beautiful forms are evolved.' I'm intrigued by this choice from the wealth of rich images in her book, but I've concluded it is an apt one, saying as much about Shepherd as the environment she is describing. Her writing often explores relationships between elements that can be both separate and united, in opposition and in harmony: '[T]he world, which is one reality, and the self, which is another reality;' a place and the mind; objects and perception; substance and spirit. Just as the battle between freezing and running water gives rise to exquisite formations, so too can the tensions between these other elements create a synthesis of beauty. The struggles Shepherd recounts are often in the effort to establish what is real, and in the dynamic exchange between inner and outer truths, a higher, more whole truth is formed: a consummation that is greater than the sum of its parts. It is a work she calls 'continuous creative act'.

In the late nineteenth and early twentieth centuries, there was a burgeoning fascination with mysticism and esoteric spiritualities in the 'west', and Shepherd was no exception. In her philosophy I recognise echoes of the prolific author and lecturer Evelyn Underhill, who explored mysticism across different religious traditions but always insisted it was practical and accessible to all. Widely read and respected at her time, she was, like Shepherd, awarded an honorary doctorate from the University of Aberdeen, so it's very likely Shepherd knew her work. 'Mysticism,' wrote Underhill, 'is the art of union with Reality.'

At the point of writing about these mountains, both Shepherd and I are in our early fifties, a transitional phase for women where changes in our bodies and our role can mean relegation to the sidelines or, on the other hand, increased freedom and possibilities. Or a mix of both. Shepherd was still working full time and caring for her chronically ill mother, but the passion of her whole-body embrace of the hills suggests it was not just a place of ease, but also of release; a place to express the wildness and sensuality that was kept in check in her professional and domestic life. But she never makes reference to this. In fact, *The Living Mountain* is fascinating in the way Shepherd says almost nothing about her life or ideas beyond the mountain, yet in taking us there through the intimacy of her bodily experience, she takes us right inside herself. She does not intend herself to be the focus. In the book she is interested in herself only to the extent that she experiences the mountain, and though we inhabit her, it is not to look into her but to look out through her eyes, to listen, feel, smell and taste through her body. Yet she is not just physical sensation; she is also mind, receiving the sensory stimuli, *feeling* them in thought and emotion and responding in words. So, the paradox, of course, is that though she tells us little about her biography, she reveals a great deal about herself. 'For as I penetrate more deeply into the mountain's life,' she writes, 'I penetrate also into my own.'

By the end of the book, have we penetrated into her life? Do we feel we know her? How do you know a person? Or a place? Or anything? These are questions that Shepherd probes throughout *The Living Mountain*. What she seeks to understand about herself is how better to know and to be one with the place, and in so doing, to ignite the inner flame of Being. In the first chapter, she writes of the mountain, '[I]t is to know its essential nature that I am seeking here. To know, that is, with the knowledge that is a process of living.' To 'know' can suggest completion or mastery, but when Shepherd speaks of 'process' she recognises an unfolding of knowledge that is never finished. 'One never quite knows the mountain, nor oneself in relation to it.' For us both, then, the writing is a journey of discovery. The difference is that when she began writing about the Cairngorms, it was after fifty years in the area and twenty-five exploring the range. I, on the other hand, begin with scant knowledge and far more limited experience – of this range, anyway. But my love of mountains is as old as my memory and so I approach these new ones in Shepherd's own belief that 'love pursued with fervour is one of the roads to knowledge'. I am hungry to know this unique landscape, to seek the hidden fires. Wherever my path will lead, my goal is the same as hers: to go higher up and deeper into the living mountain.

I.

THE GROUP

The Cairngorms were forbidden country – this was the nearest I had come to them; I was delectably excited.

Shepherd grew up fifty miles from these mountains and spoke of 'having run from childhood' in both the Deeside hills to the south-east of them and the Monadhliath range to the north-west. In *The Living Mountain* she describes the view of the Cairngorms from every angle, as if she had circumambulated the whole massif, weighing up its might against her own merits before taking the challenge. From her girlhood belief that the Cairngorms were the domain only of heroic mountaineers, her fascination for them inevitably pulled her in. The quote above comes from her first walk to their hem on a clear October day when she climbed Creag Dhubh, a low shoulder on the Spey side of the mountains, above the picturesque Loch an Eilein. She was in her mid-twenties and went alone, pushing up through the snow, thrilled, but feeling like 'a child stealing apples' for having such audacity. Her daring was rewarded. The view that opened from the top of that ridge towards the plateau in its glorious winter whites had her whooping for joy. 'From that hour I belonged to the Cairngorms . . .'

My own discovery of these mountains could not have been more different. The only similarity was our age at the time of approach. It was the summer of 1992 and, halfway through a round-the-world trip, I was spending extra time in Scotland to be with a certain Alistair, whom I'd met in Nepal. Having done his GP training in the Highlands and fallen in love with the mountains, he took me into the Cairngorms. A photo shows me on the plateau with the dark ridge of Beinn Mheadhoin behind me and Loch Etchachan a sliver of light below it. All I can recall is a long rocky walk and visiting the Shelter Stone. We must have gone up from the ski centre car park, across Cairn Gorm mountain, down the other side and then along Loch Avon to reach the Stone. It's a route Shepherd took, though I'd never heard of her then, nor anything about the Cairngorms. If I was moved or excited, I'm afraid I don't remember. There was a lot of cloud. As Shepherd herself says, 'The plateau itself is not spectacular.' Like her, the Cairngorms are not showy. It takes time, effort and love to discover their wonders, and I was yet to learn the significance of these hills. More than that, I was still bound to my first mountain range. I had just spent six months back in the Himalayas.

For much of my early childhood, our family lived in a village in the Nepal foothills, where the shining peak of Machapuchare stood like a guardian over our lives. Our home was the middle floor of a traditional house, with cattle below and grain storage above, and my favourite place was the sole window in the north wall, where I would curl up on the sill with the creaking wooden shutters pressed open and no glass blocking the cool air. From that nook, I would gaze at the sacred mountain – never climbed and now forbidden – pierced by a feeling I could not name.

When I was six, visiting friends of the family claimed that I woke them on the first morning saying, 'Come, see the mountains!' I begged to join their three-night trek up one of the Machapuchare ridges. My mother was apprehensive, but my father – who was leading it – agreed, with his characteristic belief that nothing was impossible and everyone capable of great things. Though I spent much of it cold and footsore, I was overjoyed to be included. Our first camp was in deep forest and our second above the tree-line at 13,000 feet, where I lay in the tent listening to the teenage girls talking, the 'old lady' snoring and something out in the darkness, howling. On the second morning, as we gathered snow for melting, our porters showed us prints near the camp, which they said were leopards. Shepherd writes of the sense of companionship in discovering the passage of animals. What we have lost in Britain, though, is animals whose presence brings any sense of danger. We do not like our nature too wild.

Three years later, I followed my older brother to boarding school in the hill station of Mussoorie in Uttarakhand, north India. Though only called 'hills', these Garwhal ranges rise to 8,000 feet and look north to the jagged white panorama of the Indian Himals. Hiking was a mainstay of the school programme, but the location and sprawl of the campus meant that, enthusiastic or not, we all had to hike just to get to class. In my final year, I joined a week-long trek up to the hanging valley of Har Ki Dun, requiring long, hard days carrying all our gear. The walk goes through high valleys of pine forest and alpine flower meadows beside rivers that feed the great Yamuna, twin of the Ganga. Har Ki Dun is believed by some Hindus to be the final journey of the Pandava brothers, the central characters of the Sanskrit epic, the Mahabharata. According to some versions of the legend, the last living brother ascended to heaven via the mythical stairway from the mountain Swargarohini at the valley's end. At our highest point, around 13,000 feet, surrounded by mighty peaks under a cobalt sky, with sunlight glittering off the snow, it felt like heaven had come down.

After growing up in the Himalayas, then, the mountains of Scotland did not impress. It had more to do with my ignorance than anything else, but that is often the starting point of a journey. My early hill walks in the summer of 1992 seemed invariably to involve rain and squelching through endless bog. I couldn't fathom why anyone would bother in such conditions. Why not just wait till a sunny day? I soon learned the answer to that question, but it took longer to appreciate the hills. The rate of my adjustment was closely tied to advances in my wardrobe. On my first walk, I was woefully under-equipped. Halfway through backpacking around the world, I only had thin cotton tracky bottoms, plimsolls and a fold-away mac. I remember huddling with a group of friends behind a pile of stones halfway up some ugly hill trying to eat sandwiches in the mist and drizzle, my wet trousers clinging to my legs and my fingers white with cold, failing to comprehend why on earth we were doing this.

Shepherd had grim days, too. 'For although my earliest expeditions were all made in June or July,' she wrote, 'I experienced cloud, mist, howling wind, hailstones, rain and even a blizzard.' One marvels that she kept going back. But I did too, and in no small part because of better kit. Gradually, as Alistair became fiancé and then husband, he adorned his bride with wind-and-waterproof jacket and trousers, sturdy walking boots, thermals and fleece. I learned that if I could stay warm and dry(ish), I could learn to enjoy Scottish hill walking.

I think of Shepherd's walking attire. There was no Gore-Tex or fleece back then, no multi-layer wicking fabrics or synthetic thermals, and by all accounts, she always wore skirts. For anyone who has been in the Cairngorms in winter

conditions – or even in the summer conditions she describes
– this is astonishing. But it was not so unusual at the time.
Though women were increasingly wearing trousers by the
1940s – and even shorts as early as the thirties – many
spurned them, even on hill walks, opting for woollen skirts,
jumpers and blazers, with long socks, tights, long-johns or
a slip for warmth. Tweed and tartan were popular, with
some men of the period striding up peaks in kilts, notably
the prolific writer and naturalist Seton Gordon, replete with
waistcoat, jacket, shirt, tie and hairy sporran, even when
camping. Photos suggest he could have been the gentleman
Shepherd encountered 'with eagle beak and bony knees,
descending on us out of a cloud on Ben MacDhui, kilt and
Highland cloak flapping in the rain'.

Because of its natural lanolin, wool has a degree of
water repellency, stays warm when wet and is better than
synthetic fabrics at relinquishing the odours of sweaty body
and smoky bothy. On the downside, it expands and gets
heavy with water, is harder to wash and doesn't wear well,
so has been largely replaced as an outer layer, though soft
merino is increasingly popular against the skin. Wind and
waterproofing in Shepherd's day was by virtue of waxed
cotton jackets, and footwear was either wellies or stout
workmen's boots. She quotes a teacher friend who had to
walk over rough terrain to her school every day saying, 'I
always buy men's shoes now. Nothing else is any use.' In an
essay for the *Deeside Field* magazine, Shepherd recounts her
own walk up wintry Morrone in 'ridged rubber boots on
which the snow does not cling', and in *The Living Mountain*
she is clearly wearing 'tackety beets', the Doric name for
hob-nailed boots, which were the precursor to crampons. 'In
the darkness,' she writes, 'one may touch fires from the earth
itself. Sparks fly round one's feet as the nails strike rock.'

But even when I had good boots and better clothes,

acclimatising to Scotland's hills has been a challenge. I had certainly lived in cold places and walked in snow before, but the difference here is the combination of cold, wind and wet.

The wind is always with you in the Cairngorms, like a spirit familiar. Sometimes it's just a dog nipping at your heels, at other times a flock of birds wing-beating around your head, at others, a stampede of horses knocking you over in their screaming charge. Very occasionally, it lies down and sleeps. When it does that on a below-zero day, the air around holds its breath and you can hear the ice crack. In the warmth, it's as though a soft cloak has settled over everything, stilling the leaves and the blades of grass, smoothing the loch and slowing the world to a delicious languor. In my experience, however, this is rare. In the Highlands of Scotland, particularly on the coasts and the high tops, we are a gathering of winds. Most of them blow up from the Atlantic, the trees around us beaten to a north-eastern slant, but the winds can come from any direction, bringing the bite of the North Sea or the sting of the Arctic.

Inevitably, Shepherd speaks often about them in the Cairngorms. 'The mountain makes its own wind,' she observes, describing how it 'tears across these desolate marches'. Her language bows to its brute strength: 'the mountains lashed out in whips of wind', the plateau is 'savaged', the 'terrible blasting winds' are 'bitter', 'furious' and 'ferocious'. Describing blizzards, she warns, 'It is wind that is to be feared, even more than snow itself,' and recounts the deaths that are owed to it. Nevertheless, she embraces it. In her opening lines of chapter one, she says, 'Summer on the high plateau can be delectable as honey; it can also be a roaring scourge. To those who love the place, both are good, since both are part of its essential nature.' Essential nature or not, I find the wind one of the toughest things on a Scottish hill, worse than the cold, the rain and the sleet – though worst of all in combination. It batters you, bowls you over, makes you feel in a constant fight. Could I befriend the wind? Not always, but sometimes I can lean into it with arms flung wide and let it take my weight, or run down a slope into the buffer of wind, or turn and ride its power back up the hill, literally with the wind in my sails. For embrace, that'll do.

Another essence of the mountain, often borne on the wind and to which Shepherd devotes an entire chapter, is water. Scotland is running with it. Water is everywhere, from the unfurling sky, with its leaky clouds and seeping mists, to the shape-shifting rains that can be as soft as damp breath or stinging as needles. I remember rain in Asia. I remember monsoon. Rain there could fall like the dams of the sky had broken and a torrent unleashed. I remember raindrops the size of pebbles bouncing off the ground; I remember the dusty streets of Hyderabad turning to rivers within an hour; I remember rain plastering hair and clothes to sodden skin and penetrating into travel bags and dyeing everything the colours of a bruise. Scotland does not often get these cathartic, delirious downpours but when it does, I feel a leap of excitement, standing at the door and smelling the intercourse of warm earth and wet sky; that smell called petrichor; that smell that always returns me to Asia.

They talk here of 'thin places', where the veil between earth and heaven is almost transparent, like a breath of mist or the lightest smirr of rain. It is a sense that permeates Shepherd's work. Though *The Living Mountain* is rarely explicit about spirituality, her encounter with the Cairngorms is transcendent. The stuff of nature is infused with a kind of magic, a quality and power that is half-hidden, half-sensed, but wholly essential to its being. Her writing suggests that however much the material world may be described by science, it can never be reduced to it, and that there is always more to the world – and ourselves – than meets the eye. 'The more one learns . . .' she observes, 'the more the mystery deepens.'

The idea of a 'thin place' also seems true to me of water. The membrane between dry and wet is porous and constantly breached, the air often shimmering with damp, the clouds massing and moving, mist seeping into mizzle. It makes for frequent rainbows, but also a great deal of rain. Unsurprisingly, both Gaelic and Scots are teeming with words for it. Cairngorms-based artist Amanda Thomson gathered a host of them in her visual poem 'Sixty-two words for rainy weather', made entirely of the words and their meanings. It ranges from *heavy-heartit*, for 'threatening rain', to a deluge of words all meaning 'heavy falls of rain' – *blash, plash, leesh, rasch, down-ding, trash o' weet* – to *laughing rain* that comes 'from the south west, with a clear sky line'. The poem speaks to me not just of the ubiquity of rain in its many moods but also of the resilience and humour of the people on whom it falls.

Shepherd describes water in the air in all its manifestations, from clouds that 'nuzzle (one) gently but with such persistence that (one) might as well walk through a loch' to 'the horror of walking in mist on the plateau'. For the most part, she celebrates the multitude forms of rain, which can have 'a beauty of shape and movement', but acknowledges also its darker power. 'There is a kind of rain . . . when air and ground are sodden, sullen black rain that invades body and soul alike. It gets down the neck and up the arms and into the boots. One is wet to the skin, and everything one carries has twice its weight. Then the desolation of these empty stretches of land strikes at one's heart. The mountain becomes a monstrous place.'

She talks also about the many unfathomable ways in which water inhabits the ground. 'I have seen its birth; and the more I gaze at that sure and unremitting surge of water at the very top of the mountain, the more I am baffled.' To me, much of Scotland seems saturated. In my early walking here, when I knew no better and thought I was treading on grass, I was astonished to find my feet sinking ankle deep in liquid mud. I learned the importance of waterproof boots and gaiters, but also of finding a path, or rocks, or in the absence of both, the top of a tussocky mound. I also learned that most things you sit on will give you a damp backside, often without you realising till it's too late.

In truth, there is no membrane between wet and dry but a blurring, where water seems always to be washing in and out, rising through the spongy blankets of peat and moss, trickling and pooling, drawn up into clouds, hanging in the air, swirling in mist, falling in rain, flowing and flooding. In my diary, on 2 February 2016, I wrote, 'In the past few days, Scotland was battered by a storm that tore down trees and beat rain down like bullets. Once again, the land is flooded. Even high ground seeps and weeps unable to hold more water, leaking more and more into the runnels and streams and rivers and lochs. We are awash, sodden, soaked, slipping down under the endless pull. We are drowned.' It's not for nothing that this upper part of the Spey strath where I live is called Badenoch, meaning 'the drowned lands' in Gaelic. When Shepherd writes of water, so ubiquitous, so ceaseless in its cycles, she calls it 'one of the four elemental mysteries' and 'like all profound mysteries, it is so simple that it frightens me'.

Something about the wet seems to carry the cold deeper into my body. Or perhaps it is just age, but every winter I get the itchy heat of chilblains in my fingers and toes, and even in summer, Raynaud's syndrome turns them purple, blue and white. At a barbecue beside Loch Morlich one July, when the wind off the loch was merciless, a friend wrapped a down jacket around me as I stood clutching a burger in skeleton hands with my teeth rattling. Sometimes I feel I've spent the whole winter with my shoulders hunched to my ears and my chest caved in. Shepherd, by contrast, strikes me as staggeringly hardy, facing down the cold with good Scottish stoicism and even relishing it. Visitors found her house chilly and claimed she often couldn't be bothered to light a fire. Her references to cold in *The Living Mountain* acknowledge sharpness, but in a way that enlivens. 'Cold spring water stings the palate, the throat tingles unbearably; cold air smacks the back of the mouth, the lungs crackle.' She describes barefoot fording of snow-melt streams as 'icy delight' and glories in plunging into freezing lochs. She rarely complains about feeling too cold to enjoy the outdoors, and that first walk to the edge of the Cairngorms she recounts as 'blue, cold and brilliant'.

So, I spent the first few years of my life in Scotland learning how to withstand the weather, how to find enough clothes to keep it out, how to fend off the wind and the rain and the frostbite while I peered at the landscape from under the tightly drawn flap of my hood. But slowly, slowly, I have moved from embattled defence through grudging accommodation to acceptance and even, yes, embrace. I was going to say truce, but that would suggest movement and compromise on both sides. Unlike me, the weather remains unchanged. No, that is not right, either, for the weather is changing. But not to favour me. It is unconscious and blind to my personal experience; it does not accommodate me nor adjust to function better alongside me, as I must do for it. It is element and force, not sentient being. However much we may personify it, feeling by turns attacked or blessed, it does not think or know or relate. 'It does nothing,' as Nan Shepherd says of water, 'absolutely nothing, but be itself.'

The journey, then, and the surrender, is all mine.

Nearly thirty years after my first Cairngorms walk, I retrace Shepherd's fateful steps up Creag Dubh. I do not go alone, as she did, because it is midwinter and I lack the navigation and technical skills to be safe. My companion, now merged with my identity as much as with the mountain, is still Alistair. The name of the hill means 'black crag' in Gaelic, but on the early December day we go, its slopes are lost in white cloud, the earth sodden and the skies heavy. Nevertheless, it is exciting. Not only am I following her journey, but also discovering Creag Fhiaclach, one of the last remaining stands of montane scrub in this fragment of ancient Caledonian forest. We leave the path to cut across uneven ground, humpy with snow-laden heather. Here are spiky, fragrant junipers, Scots pines with red bark and needles of unfailing green, and birch, their lichened trunks rising through a haze of purple branches, beaded with water droplets.

Like Shepherd, we 'toil' up the slope, slower with each snow-sinking step. But unlike her, we do not reach the breath-catching view of the Cairngorms plateau. Instead, we walk deeper and deeper into mist. By the time we reach the scrub, the dwarf trees appear like the ghosts of departed bonsai. We hear red grouse gurgling but see only their prints and two drifting feathers. Checking map, compass and aspect of slope, we climb higher, till even the rocks disappear and there is nothing on the black crag but white.

No seam now between sky and snow, up or down, here or there. No borders, no boundaries. Has this place become 'thin' or impenetrably thick? Tiny brown tendrils flicker across my vision and disappear like smoke. I am dizzy. For a moment we believe the cloud might dissolve to a singing blue sky, but a hard stare renders only blankness. When Shepherd gained the top, she 'jumped up and down . . . laughed and shouted'. We will save that for another day. It has taken too long to get this far already, and we must turn home before the short day turns dark. As we plough slowly back, knee deep and led by the voice of a hidden stream, the lightest motes of snow begin to fall.

II.

FROST & SNOW

*One walks among elementals, and elementals
are not governable. There are awakened also
in oneself by the contact elementals that are as
unpredictable as wind or snow.*

The Cairngorms in winter are a landscape of as much treachery as beauty. In *The Living Mountain*, Shepherd describes how local folk – hill farmers, keepers and estate labourers – condemned winter climbing as irresponsible, but nevertheless were selfless when rescue was required. 'If a man does not come back, they go out to search for him with patience, doggedness and skill, often in appalling weather conditions; and when there is no more hope of his being alive, seek persistently for the body.' In her foreword thirty years later, one of the changes she notes is the establishment and 'magnificent work' of the Mountain Rescue. She also acknowledges the lives lost, including what has become known as the Cairngorms Plateau Disaster in 1971, where five school pupils and one of their instructors died. Considered Britain's worst mountaineering accident, the event spurred stricter standards for school trips and greater resource for Rescue Teams. Exacting high levels of experience, training and organisation, the teams operate at a professional level, responding to call-outs year-round in some of the most dangerous circumstances, with missions that can extend over several days. Despite these demands, all team members are volunteers. What is clear from their experience and all the writing about the Cairngorms, from Nan Shepherd to John Allen's *Cairngorm John: A Life in Mountain Rescue*, is that this range is far more challenging than most people realise.

From the temperate valleys, and particularly in comparison with the Himals, they look innocuous enough: gently rolling hills that can be topped in a few hours. 'Given clear air, and the unending daylight of a Northern summer,' wrote Shepherd, 'there is not one of the summits but can be reached by a moderately strong walker without distress.' Many people imagine they can stroll up one of the built paths on a sunny day, take in the view and amble back down with little more than sandals and a water bottle. Many people try it. Not many try it again, because the reality is much harsher. Hidden within the mountain's green folds, the cliffs are steep and the scree slopes unstable. Many of the routes have no clear path, and to the inexperienced Cairngorm walker, the plateau may seem to have few distinguishing features, making navigation by sight unreliable. More critically, favourable conditions may not last the day or the distance, even in summer. As the largest area of high ground in Britain, the Cairngorms have little buffer from the winds sweeping in from the oceans that make it a 'region of swift and unpredictable change'. The balmy warmth of the valley can disappear on the tops, with winds adding chill and dangerous gusts. The highest speed recorded on top of Cairngorm is 176 miles per hour. Heather Morning, who has served as Mountain Safety Adviser for Mountaineering Scotland and on the Cairngorms Mountain Rescue Team, has a simple formula for calculating the effect of wind-speed on walkers: each ten miles per hour is equivalent to a pint of beer. Gusts of anything over seventy miles per hour mean most people are, as they say, legless. I can testify. Having struggled up an exposed ridge in sixty-mile-per-hour winds, I had to hunker down and brace with both hands through each gust.

Shepherd doesn't comment on her drinking habits but does agree that 'Man is not in his element in air that moves at this velocity'. She also watches a bank of cloud 'blotting out a hundred summits a minute'. This can plunge walkers into a white-out before they've had time to get their bearings. The dangers are exacerbated in winter, with the extremes of wind and cold, the short hours of daylight and the inscrutable behaviour of snow. Storms brew, blizzards rise, avalanches fall. It is part of what makes the Cairngorms such a wild and endlessly changing place, but also why, as Shepherd puts it, they are 'not to be undertaken lightly'. Along with her, I have learned that going into these mountains, especially in winter, requires alertness and preparation.

My first plan for a winter skills course with Mountaineering Scotland in January 2020 was dashed by the combination of my heavy cold and Storm Brendan. My mountain guide friend, John Lyall, generously offered to take me out in February, but before we could go, we were hit by Storm Ciara, which smashed wind and rain across the UK, flooding some communities and disrupting travel everywhere. Hard on her heels came Storm Dennis, one of the most intense extra-tropical cyclones to that date and the thirteenth of the European windstorm season. That makes it sound like a champions' league of the weather gods, but the results are always climactic hooliganism and no winners. Even before Covid became a global pandemic, the year was not shaping up well.

We'd made plans for the training on the Monday after Dennis, but John came round in a blur of snow on the Sunday afternoon. 'Forecast for tomorrow is winds of seventy to a hundred miles per hour on the mountain,' he said, stamping his boots in our porch. Seven to ten pints of beer. To my vast relief, he advised postponing and we settled down by the roaring fire with tea and chocolate ginger biscuits. John is something of a Nan Shepherd of the climbing world, doing absolutely nothing to promote himself. He has no website or social media and his entry on the official British Mountain Guide site is blank apart from a photo of a marmot. The one on the Mountain Training site has no photo and, other than a list of qualifications, states, *This person has not written a profile yet. This person has not written a story yet. This person has no connections.*

Nothing could be further from the truth. John is one of the most experienced and highly respected British Mountain Guides in Scotland, a member of the International Federation of Mountain Guides Associations, with forty years on the Cairngorms Mountain Rescue Team. He has guided internationally from the Himalayas to South America to Greenland and has featured in BBC television programmes including *A Year in the Wild*, about the Cairngorms. He has never advertised, in print or online, preferring word-of-mouth recommendations and always having enough work. At time of writing, though, the wide reach of his guiding had drawn into an ever-smaller circle around the needs of his ninety-three-year-old mother, living with encroaching dementia. A wife of the manse, she used to give passing vagrants a cup of tea and a bite to eat. Inspired, the young John decided being a tramp was his life's ambition, wandering freely – as he saw it – and finding kindness along the way. Shepherd would have approved, admitting to being a shameless 'vagabond . . . a peerer into corners'. Like her, John's tramping was curtailed by the care of a mother, though unlike her, he was also the resident housekeeper and needed to be with his mother most of the time. When we visited them in the back garden, it was the tramp making the coffee and passing biscuits to the lady. Eyes shining, she told me of her own love for the hills and how she'd been the one to coax her late husband into the Cairngorms.

* * *

A month after our fireside conversation, John gives a day of his precious respite time to take me up the mountain. On this occasion, the weather has opened to sunshine and very little wind, and I am all too aware of my blessings. Donning our kit in the car park, we watch flocks of snow buntings gather on the picnic tables, small ovals of white blushed with rust at head and throat, wings a flutter of browns. They are one of the remarkable birds that survive the Cairngorms through the winter. 'Both in song and in person,' wrote Shepherd, 'these small creatures have a delicate perfection that is enhanced by the savagery of their home.' We head to the ranger base, where John talks me through the weather and avalanche information screens. He has studied these forecasts and their outcomes in detail for many years, now reading the patterns of sky and snow like a prophet. Stalling the vagrancy dream, he originally trained as a forester, and as we head around the hill, he tells me about the trees. Most of the Cairngorm slopes at this level and above are bare, but in the gully leading up to Coire an t-Sneachda, there is a scattering of Scots pine trees, stunted and scruffy. Shepherd described ones like these: 'Some of these out-liers show the amazing adaptability of this tree. They can change their form at need, like any wizard.'

It was John's forestry research in the early 1980s that revealed these juvenile-looking specimens to be around ninety to a hundred years old. Scots pine seeds are generally too heavy to blow far and are completely digested when eaten, so not carried in animal droppings. Certain rare winter conditions mean water around the seeds freezes, making them smooth, and the strong winds send them rolling across the surface of packed snow till they settle in vegetation high up on wind-scoured slopes, to defrost and germinate. The extreme environment, however, means their growth is incredibly slow and most remain low and spreading, rather than upright. They are vulnerable because of their wide spacing, and damaged by frost, wind burn and the rubbing of deer antlers against the bark. But they cling on. By contrast, beside the path lies a huge, bleached Scots pine root stump, preserved in peat and probably 2,000 years old, a testament to a different climate and the size and strength of the trees that once grew at this altitude.

Walking on, John tells me about the rocks. It takes me back to a Grade 6 science project in India where we had to assemble and identify a rock collection. I was useless. They all looked the same to me: equally grey, mottled and dull. I labelled the lot 'conglomerate' and ended my geology career. Rocks failed to interest me for a very long time until a walk in the Himalayas where our guide pointed out the imprint of sea creatures in the stone. When he explained that these mountains had once been under the ocean, my mind spun. Till then, rocks not only looked boring but never did anything. Here, at last, was journey. Here was story.

My appreciation of the Scottish hills also underwent a seismic shift when I learned that these are some of the oldest rocks on Earth: the Lewisian Gneiss of the west coast and Western Isles dates back over three billion years. The Cairngorms, in the heart of Scotland, are not gneiss but mainly granite, what Sheperd called 'this grumbling, grinding mass of plutonic rock'. The story begins 700 million years ago in Dalradian sediments at the bottom of the Iapetus Ocean. The sediments are named for the early

Gaelic kingdom of Dál Riada and the ocean for the mythic
Greek titan, son of Uranus and father of Atlas, for whom
the Atlantic is named. Over eons of time, the colliding of
vast continents pushed the Iapetus down and the land up,
metamorphosing and deforming the rock in the geological
event called the Caledonian Orogeny. This was 425 million
years ago and created an enormous range of Himalayan
proportions stretching from what is now southern Norway,
across Scotland and into the Appalachian mountains.
Though at 1,300 metres the rounded Cairngorm hills today
are only a fraction of Everest, at 8,848 metres, at that time,
they were possibly taller. Deep down below those towering
peaks, the increasing pressure of tectonic plates forced
plumes of magma to rise and crystallise very slowly in the
Earth's crust. This became the Cairngorms granite, a rock so
tough that even after the kilometres of Dalradian mountain
above were eroded away, it has endured. In turn weathered
by ice, wind, water and stone, through freezing and fire, the
range has been sculpted into its distinctive flowing shapes
with its hollowed corries and hidden ravines. As Shepherd
knew, 'Thirty years in the life of a mountain is nothing.'
Now when I look at the Cairngorms, I see the slumbering
giants of time.

More than their age, I was impressed to discover that
these mountains are also migrants. Far back in the geological
past, the landmass that included Scotland was drifting near
the South Pole and wandered from the southern hemisphere
through all the climactic zones of the earth before settling
in its current location. During its nomadic existence, like
a great ark of stone, it harboured a giant and changing
menagerie of animals in a constantly evolving environment.
This land moved from ocean floor to blistering deserts,
tropical jungles to ice-bound mountains. As a result, no
other country of its size has as varied a geology and range of

landscapes as Scotland. I find it fascinating to contemplate the passage of land on this tremendous scale. We typically think of it as the solid base, the fixed point, the 'terra firma' over which plants, animals and people come and go. Some of us claim levels of ownership, while others think more in terms of belonging. But there is a whole new perspective when we recognise land itself as a traveller. Even millions of years after these mountains settled at 57 degrees latitude and lost their upper ranges, they kept on moving. Ice clawed across this landscape, smashing and splitting the rocks into new patterns, dragging some many miles from home, leaving others in tiers and terraces. As successive freezes came and went, water cut its own swathe in rivers and lakes, so that by the time ice cover had left Scotland by 10,000 BCE, the larger moulding of the Cairngorms was complete. Today, they encompass an exceptionally diverse range of landforms.

Shepherd apprehends something of the mountain's ancient and ongoing movement through one of her exercises in shifting perception. 'Moving the eye itself when looking at things that do not move, deepens one's sense of outer reality. Then static things may be caught in the very act of becoming.' In a moment of studied contemplation, she kaleidoscopes space and time and homes in on the whole point for her: to penetrate to the essence, the truth of the matter. And even though Shepherd knew the textbook information about these mountains and includes some of it in *The Living Mountain*, on page one she says it 'is a pallid simulacrum of their reality'. From the outset, she seeks to move past external descriptors to actual, direct encounter. She goes on to provide a written record of her own, but one that insists the character of the mountain is not fixed but living and changing and always beyond our capacity to fully know. Even the rock.

John and I pause to observe the differences between the

Cairngorms granite and the vestiges of the older Dalradian schists that once covered the range but are mainly limited to the fringes. These usually appear in fragmentary tide-lines around the hills, where they have been dumped by glacial action, and are darker and smoother with ingrained lines, whereas the granite is speckled. Lichens grow on both rocks, but the bright orange ones only on the schist. The green lichens on the grey granite give the hills their blueish tone in certain light, explaining the Gaelic name Cairngorm from *càrn gorm*: 'blue hill' (though *gorm* can also mean 'green'). The name of this one summit was applied to the whole range by outsiders at some point in the late eighteenth century and has not only stuck but extended to embrace the surrounding area as well. Of the Cairngorms granite, Shepherd wrote, 'Crags, boulders and scree alike are weathered to a cold grey, but find the rock where it is newly slashed, or under water, and there is the glow of the red.' The combination of freshly exposed granite after a landslip and the russet shades of heather in the sun probably account for the original Gaelic name for the whole range, Am Monadh Ruadh: The Red Hills.

Today, they are white. The site for our training will be Coire an t-Sneachda: the Corrie of the Snow. An amphitheatre of cliffs curves around a rocky hollow, pillowed, quilted, heaped in pure white. There are climbers going up the steep gullies and skiers coming back down what appear to be near-vertical sweeps. On the cliff tops, the snow juts out in cornices where puffs of wind toss it in flurries against the azure sky. A raven makes its ragged black flight from the rocks with a guttural croak. Here on the ground, there is a rippling in the snow that evokes the fine ridges on a beach or the fish-scale pattern of clouds. Low, soft wind swifts over the surface like a spirit, a fleeting breath of snow, lithe and shape-shifting before it vanishes into air. At our feet, several boot shapes rise in inverted prints. These are made by the packed-down snow under the boot holding its form when the lighter snow is blown away. Animal steps can be elevated in the same way, and the smallest reverse print John has seen is the pencil thin claw of a snow bunting. Delighted by such animal tracks, Shepherd reflected, 'One is companioned, though not in time.'

Like the rock, snow has a journey and a story. Not only does John's work as a guide require him to predict the future, but also to divine the past. He reads the snow like lifelines across the mountain's palm, scanning its colours and patterns, plunging his ice axe into a bank and inspecting the granules on his glove. Adding these to his scouring of the weather charts from previous weeks, he pieces together its fate. The history of snow is shaped by infinite inter-connecting factors: the changing weather conditions, even within one day; the temperature fluctuations; the speed and direction of the levels of moisture in the air and its precipitation; the movements of water, ice and snow from high to low and back again; and the altitude, aspect and gradient of the ground on which it lands. It is a highly complex web of events but in the mountains, learning to read the snow is key to safe passage across it.

Gradually, like invisible ink materialising on pale parchment, its text emerges. All around us is wind-slab snow, white, creamy and a bit sticky, blown into place and not packed down, seductive but unstable. The older snow is more blue-green or silver, and learning to recognise it reminds me of Shepherd's eye for the many colours of snow depending on formation and light. Nothing is just black and white to her; she sees slopes of snow 'washed in blaeberry' or 'golden green' or 'burning with a vivid electric blue'. As well as variations of colour, snow has myriad textures. A scattering of tiny white balls like Styrofoam is graupel, what people sometimes mistake for hail but are actually snow crystals rimed with frozen water droplets. John cuts through a bank of snow to reveal its layers, not unlike an archaeological dig. The deeper snow has glints of green and there are seams that sparkle. He presses into it to test the hardness and identifies strips of 'depth hoar', an ice crystal layer low down which is a fault line where an avalanche is likely to fall away. There is an old saying: 'Don't go out during or twenty-four hours after snowfall.' Shepherd says, '[T]he gamekeeper's dictum is: if you can't see your own footsteps behind you in the snow, don't go on.' In fact, John warns me, it can be risky at any time.

* * *

I look out across the undulating expanse of snow around me, at the singing sky. It is what locals call a 'bluebird day'. John and I walked here without jackets and are sitting in the sunshine eating sandwiches; everything appears serene and safe. It looks like the time when Shepherd 'walked all day through millions of sparkling sun spangles on the frosty snow'. I am learning, as she so often points out, how deceptive appearances can be. It is why I am here to gain winter skills, that I may walk safely into the serenity. And now the easy bit is over: the path, the looking and talking, the packed lunch. Now I must throw myself down the mountain.

The prospect of this has twisted inside me like a dark snake from the moment I bought my first ice axe two months ago. I'd had no intention of taking up climbing, certainly not in winter, so hadn't thought I would need one. In all my snowy walking of the past I'd never had an axe, or even crampons. Looking back, much of that walking had been on clear paths or in mild conditions, and – in truth – I should have been better equipped. I don't know what I imagined I would do if I fell down a slope, but I certainly hadn't conjured stunts with a metal pick. Nan Shepherd hadn't warned me, either. But John is clear. 'I will teach you how to do this, but I hope you never have to use it. If you learn to walk properly, you never will.'

Part of that walking in winter involves awareness of every step, 'the senses keyed', as Shepherd describes it. We make our way up the slope, kicking a level ledge for each boot-fall. For experienced mountaineers, it becomes instinctive, but for beginners it means consciously noting where and how you put your feet and your weight, depending on the conditions of the snow, the gradient, the fall line and the landscape around. We reach a spot where John hollows out a seat in the slope. Perched in it, he explains the technique of an ice axe arrest, pushes off cheerfully and performs the manoeuvre with a dancer's grace. My stomach churns. The worst moment for me is wriggling into position in the hollow, looking down the sheer snow and thinking about it. I say aloud each thing I have to remember, in more-or-less the right order, though several things are supposed to happen at the same time: *grab spike, roll, feet up, face away, arch body, dig axe in under shoulder, come to elegant stop.* Deep breath and I push off. Cue frantic fumbling, face turned the wrong way, feet ploughing into the snow and me skeetering down with the axe dragging well above me. I do stop, mercifully, though mainly because of the natural friction of my jacket. (I am never parting with this jacket.) I am alive. John is smiling.

A fall down the mountain is never going to be choreographed or start from a comfortable seat moments after you have rehearsed the steps. So, John takes me through ice axe arrest from different positions: feet first on my back, feet first on my stomach, then lying on my stomach and hurtling down head-first. Never fond of rollercoasters, it is all gut-wrenching stuff for me, though I am gradually getting the moves and managing to slow my breathing. And then he has his Nan Shepherd moment. Sitting in the hollow facing the mountain, he lies back, head down the slope, and waxes lyrical about her description of seeing the world upside down. 'How new it has become!' I want to point out that she was standing on solid ground at the time and merely peering through her legs. (She categorically *never* mentions ice axe practice. No mention of ice axes at all, for that matter.) After John has glided through his inverted arrest, I take the hollow, say an inner prayer for courage and lie back. My heart stops. The world hangs above space; at the top, a cathedral dome of snow and rock, then frescoes of forested valleys and lochs, all suspended above an emptiness of blue. It is so striking and beautiful it triumphs over my fear and stills me. Then comes the strangest feeling of sliding on my back down a snow bank, swift and free, childlike. Unafraid. Not just the world, but I, too, have become new.

And that is another leaf I take from Shepherd's book: to come to the mountain like a child. To experience it with the playfulness and total, full-bodied presence of the very young, before the clarity of our encounters have been clouded by history, assumptions, pre-occupations and analysis. The route to this direct engagement, suggests Shepherd, is through the senses. 'Each sense heightened to its most exquisite awareness, is in itself total experience. This is the innocence we have lost.' It chimes with the mystic Evelyn Underhill. 'What is it, then, which distinguishes the outlook of great poets and artists . . .? Innocence and humility distinguish it. These persons prejudge nothing . . . their attitude to the universe is that of children; and because this is so, they participate to that extent in the Heaven of Reality.' I've heard this somewhere before. *Truly I tell you, unless we change and become like little children, we will never enter the kingdom of heaven.*

Heading across the bowl of the corrie we stop at the permanent Mountain Rescue equipment box and John inspects the contents. The size of two baths stacked on top of each other, it is made of steel and took twenty team members to carry into position. It holds stretchers, casualty bags, shovels and avalanche probes and is kept unlocked for ease of access in the corrie most beloved of climbers but also most notorious in the Cairngorms for accidents. In Shepherd's 'Frost and Snow' chapter, she dedicates two pages to recounting lives lost in winter conditions, and for all her delight in the mountains, she never romanticises them or underplays their danger. 'It is the risk we must all take when we accept individual responsibility for ourselves on the mountain, and until we have done that, we do not begin to know it.' Here is another way of knowing, which seems the opposite of being child-like: assessing risk and taking responsibility. Yet in a book exploring mysteries, she touches here on one of the most profound: how it can be that those who love life so much can risk it so readily. For to undertake adventure is not just a sign of love for the thing explored – the mountain, the ocean, the desert – but for life itself. To extend oneself to such heights and depths 'intensifies life to the point of glory'.

And at the same time, it threatens it. It is what she explores in the old Scottish word *fey*. 'One is raised; fey; a little mad, in the eyes of the folk who do not climb.' The term carries not just hints of delirium, but also destruction. How 'a man may seem to walk securely over dangerous places with the gay abandon that is said to be the mark of those who are doomed to death'. And yet, as she explains, for mountain-goers with knowledge – both theoretical and lived – it is not 'gay abandon'. It is learning, experience, skill. And, yes, the acceptance of risk. Paradoxically, for many, it is the sharp-edge of danger that actually makes the going

– and the living – worthwhile. It gives bite and energy; it summons power. And in those who truly know, humility. John has lifted injured people from ice-crusted ledges, drawn struggling climbers up to cliff tops or lowered them to rocky beds, held the wounded and fallen, carried the dead. It has not diminished his love of mountains or his passion for guiding others, but it has deepened his wisdom. And for all the people who wander mountains, relatively few are lost. There is far more madness and death from despair in our settlements than in our wilderness. To go beyond the self is to find the self.

* * *

The time has come to learn the kind of walking that should negate the need for ice axe arrest. The time for crampons. Shepherd doesn't mention these, either, but rather the boots with nails that worked nearly as well. I had practised putting my crampons on and off at home, in case I would need to do it in wind and whirling snow. Today the weather is kind, but I keep my inner gloves on through the fiddly positioning and threading of the ties. John advises tucking gloves into your jacket as soon as you remove them, and always having three pairs in winter; he recalls helping a lone Russian woman struggling across the frozen mountain bare-handed, gloves blown away.

'Now you have lethal weapons on your feet,' he says calmly as I straighten up. 'Never walk normally in crampons, never forget you're wearing them.' In order to have the necessary grip for winter conditions, the points are sharp enough to rip fabric and flesh and are the reason you must keep feet up when sliding down a slope. If they dig into the snow, they will stick while the rest of your body plummets on, probably breaking a leg in the process. We go through the John Wayne gait and all the ways of getting across snow, rock and ice; the hardest part for me is heading straight down a rock slope, smooth with its skin of ice, while fighting the urge to break into a run. My leg muscles burn.

As clouds gather, we head up the steep snowy side of the corrie, using both ice axe and crampons for purchase, taking each step at a time, sometimes flat-footed, sometimes front-pointing straight into the slope. It is slow going, but I am drawn into the steady, conscious interaction of body, equipment and elements. The totality of focus is both challenging and calming. Nothing else comes to mind; nothing else matters. It is what Shepherd observes about the climber's experience: 'What he values is a task that, demanding of him all he has and is, absorbs and so releases him entirely.'

We come out onto the western ridge, and look across the spill of mountains around us, metallic and shining. To the south, the clouds are pale gold with the lowering sun while, far above, they give way to the remaining fragments of blue. The rocks on the ridge are fringed with rime ice. This forms when water droplets in a cold wind freeze on contact with the rock and gradually build into patterns of feather and lace, some pure white, others clear as glass. I see one clinging to the rock by the tiniest hold but supporting a long span of ice, suspended in the air. Here is both the antiquity and impermanence of the mountain; its longevity and fragility. On a rock that took shape 400 million years ago, surviving ice and fire and eons of time, hangs a water crystal, blown on wind from the Atlantic yesterday, lost tomorrow in snow.

As we crunch down the ridge, the lights of the valley twinkling in the pools of dusk, I ask John, of all the world's mountain ranges he has walked, which does he love the most? I already know the answer. He gestures around him, shaking his head with a wry smile, as if I could not possibly fathom it. It is like Shepherd, who said, 'However

often I walk on them, these hills hold astonishment for me.'
For John, they hold the dark-night blizzards of Mountain
Rescue, the falling of friends to their death, the frozen body
of a child; but they hold also the struggle and the saving, the
life stretched large by a mountain's life, the call of beauty
and the mystery of faith. And across these ancient slopes, the
footfall of a beloved mother, who still remembers.

III.

THE PLATEAU

*The high plateau where these streams begin, the
streams themselves, their cataracts and rocky
beds, the corries, the whole wild enchantment,
like a work of art is perpetually new when one
returns to it.*

'The Plateau' was the title Shepherd originally chose for
the entire book, and it was Neil Gunn who suggested
she find a better one. She clearly did but retained 'The Plateau'
as her first chapter, which is interesting to me. No experience
of the Cairngorms starts at the top. There is always the
journey up, which Shepherd describes in terms that range
from 'toiling' to 'running'. There is also no chapter in the
book titled 'Summit' because she maintains 'the plateau is
the true summit of these mountains'. So why did she start her
book – which is so profoundly about a journey of discovery
– at the top? I wonder if it is a deliberate inversion of the
traditional mountain climbing tale that places the summit
at the climax of the story: the destination, the high point
around which the rest of the narrative arc curves. Perhaps,
also, she is acknowledging it was her own initial drive.
Her first climb was up Ben Macdui, the highest. After that,
'mad to recover the tang of height, I made always for the

summits'. Gradually, she relinquished the race to 'the horrid pinnacle' and started to explore the recesses, the lochs and burns, flowers and birds. So, although the literal journey to the mountain starts at the bottom, her experience and her narrative starts at the top and works its way down and in. 'At first I was seeking only sensuous gratification – the sensation of height, the sensation of movement,' she explains. 'But as I grew older and less self-sufficient, I began to discover the mountain in itself.'

For me, also, the plateau has been the ground of beginnings. My first walk across it – the one with Alistair in 1992 – was my first hill walk in Scotland. It is also the place I began learning to ski. Listing the changes on Cairngorm in her foreword, Shepherd describes skiers that are 'swift, elate, controlled, miracles of grace and precision . . .' She was not describing me. I am the kind of figure on whom the cartoonists base their sketches; the hapless character slamming into trees, upended in the snow or shooting off cliffs. If only it were so funny at the time. I didn't start learning till my late thirties and, despite some lessons from the excellent local instructors, never really mastered the art. I partly blame the mountain, where the conditions can be so atrocious that you are bent double in the wind, ice stinging your face and the flat white of snow and cloud bringing vertigo. People say that if you can ski on Cairngorm, you can ski anywhere. It reminds me of Shepherd's hillwalking experience in Galloway, southern Scotland. A local shepherd met her request for directions with scepticism, asking if she knew what she was undertaking. When she explained she'd been all over the Cairngorms, his response was unequivocal: '"The Cairngorms, have you?" His gesture dismissed me – it was like a drawbridge thrown forward.'

I have yet to test my supposed Cairngorms prowess at any other ski location, and I am yet to give up. Shepherd's description of skiers includes those who 'flounder – but all with exhilaration'. I confess my floundering has not always been with such high spirits, but in spite of the freezing and frustrations, there are days up on the plateau on skis that have been, even for me, a taste of glory. There's no evidence of Shepherd skiing herself, but she spent time up on the tops in all weathers and was intoxicated by it. Of the plateau, she said, '[O]ne has the sense of being lifted, as on a mighty shelf, above the world.'

The Cairngorms are such an unusual mountain range because of this wide space at the top. Most mountains get narrower and sharper as they go up, and harder to traverse, while most plateaus are merely an elevated plain or tableland, but not normally called 'mountains'. The village of my childhood in Nepal sprawled across a sloping plateau rising above the Seti River, but it was only an apron extending to the foothills, in turn reaching up to the high, white peaks of the Annapurnas. Though the Cairngorms are in some places bounded and intersected by steep cliffs, they open out at the top in an undulating carpet with relatively modest rises and falls. This is partly why Shepherd insists 'they must be seen as a single mountain'. Certainly, the hardest slog is to get up to the plateau, but once on it, there are acres of easy wandering, an extended experience of elevation and, from the rim, views that can travel to the edges of Scotland. 'On a clear day,' Shepherd claims, 'one looks without any sense of strain from Morven in Caithness to the Lammermuirs, and out past Ben Nevis to Morar.' What's more, it is a striking environment, because unlike the snow-bound summits of the Himalayas and Alps, the plateau shifts through a wide range of conditions from sweet, summery balm to arctic blizzard. Every visit is a first.

* * *

In late March 2020, a few days after my winter skills training with John, Alistair and I took our golden retriever, Sileas, up the mountain. The sky that day was a mass of brooding clouds in every shade of grey, the snow surface hard. Because of Covid, it had been declared the last day of skiing and the car park was busy, though nothing like the usual numbers for that time of year. Hoping to get to Ben Macdui – from the opposite side to Shepherd's approach – we set off on the path, practising my embryonic navigational skills. Then with crampons strapped and ice axes wielded, we struck up the snowy slope, a stiff wind slowing us down but gradually opening the sky. Fragments of snow blew over the frozen surface with a skeetering sound like crab claws, and as the sun broke through, the surface patterns stood out in sharp relief: the ripples and pockles, the glassy sweeps, the powder-soft piles. We were still low enough that the expanse of white was speckled with black rocks, like the coat of a Dalmatian. Sheltering behind one of the bigger boulders for coffee and sandwiches, we stopped for so long it made me cold, and Alistair commented that winter walkers often eat on the move.

Emerging onto the plateau, the sky had turned blue and innocent, its clouds now picture-book fluffy, but the wind was still strong and we were behind time. It is so often the way with winter walking. Everything takes longer. All that faffing with layers and kit, all those steps sinking into snow or cutting a way, all that peering at maps and the misleading landscape. 'For not getting lost is a matter of the mind,' wrote Shepherd, 'of keeping one's head, of having map and compass to hand and knowing how to use them.' We knelt down to study ours – like gloves, maps are prone to blow away in the wind – and agreed that Ben Macdui, 'the giant he is', was now too ambitious, so we changed plan to head straight back along the top of the Northern Corries to Cairn Gorm and the car park.

Sileas didn't care where we were going, so long as she could come, leading the charge, if possible. She loves snow, leaping and tumbling in it, jumping to catch it in her mouth and rolling on her back like it's the best possible massage. As we climbed higher, the wind blew her amber fur into a corona and her ridiculously happy face gradually wizened with frosted whiskers and brows. She sometimes slipped on the steeper snow and ventured too close to cornices, so we had to keep calling her back, especially when tossed dog snacks flew away on the wind and she chased them, heedless of cliff edges. Later we saw three men swifting down the ski slopes with a lithe greyhound in a smart tartan coat, keeping pace in wild joy. Dogs certainly know the exhilaration of which Shepherd wrote; the mystics often advise learning from animals for the fuller life.

The plateau was radiant sunshine, and we could see down into Coire an t-Sneachda, where I had turned upside down with an ice axe just days before, on into the wooded valley of Glenmore and across Loch Morlich with its skirt of hills, to the smoky blue Monadhliaths in the west. At that altitude, the snow was a deep layer of royal icing, but changing with every angle and slope: in some places slick and glossy as fresh paint, in others a burnished silver, in others, the texture of rough, raw silk. We could see the tops of the range on all sides, the swan-back curves and sweeps broken by dark crags, the bright shoulders and blue shadows, the high lochs quilted in white. Any exposed rocks were captive to frost, a build-up of snow blown round their backs and the fingers of rime ice reaching straight into the south-westerly wind. Above us, the sky slowly turned to a creamy mother-of-pearl, harbouring all the tints of rose, fawn and grey, translucent clouds suspended like fragments of muslin. Here was a world shaped to a beauty both fleeting and eternal. In Shepherd's words: 'I knew when I had looked for a long time that I had hardly begun to see.'

By the time we arrived home, it was to the news that Mountain Rescue and Mountaineering Scotland were asking people not to go up hills for the foreseeable future. It was our last Cairngorm walk of that winter and spring.

* * *

The next time we could return to the plateau was 1 June and a day at the opposite end of the weather spectrum, one that Shepherd would call 'delectable as honey'. This time we were on the western side of the Lairig Ghru, the ravine that cuts north–south through the range, and it was my first time climbing Braeriach. It's a great beast of a hill, long and hulking with gaping corries gouged from its sides and rock-shattered precipices plunging from its rim. The name means 'brindled upland' in Gaelic and hints at the many faces, colours and moods of this inscrutable mountain. It can be dappled in greens and browns, or glowing red in the setting sun, or a haze of indigo. But also there are times when it is black with storm, or strafed by rain, and whole days when it descends into a weary grey or completely vanishes in cloud. Some of the most harrowing accounts of blizzard and blind stumbling in the Cairngorms come from Braeriach. In W.H. Murray's transporting work *Mountaineering in Scotland*, he describes having to 'crawl on hands and knees over the last twenty yards to the cairn, for we were unwilling to be picked up and hurled down the Lairig Ghru face'. So, on my first ascent of the great mountain, I could barely believe how benign she was, stretched out languidly in summer warmth, her flanks washed with light.

Of all the high tops of the Cairngorms, the plateau

of Braeriach seems distinct. Shepherd spoke of its arctic qualities in the clarity of air and the tenacity and loveliness of its flowers. The naturalist Seton Gordon, who was the first to document the ecology of the Cairngorms in depth and whom Shepherd cites, likened it to the tundra of Spitsbergen, Norway. Of a July day in 1923, he wrote, 'One saw the same gentle slopes, with lingering snowfields gleaming white, the same plants that crept prostrate or formed a dense stunted growth to shield them from the fierce winds that play here. There was the same exhilarating air, tense and vital.' The day of our own summer expedition, the plateau unfurled around us, wide and rolling like a grassy sea, with not a breath of wind. I don't think I'd ever felt such a stillness in the air so high in the Cairngorms, or such a capacity to stroll or sit or stretch out as the whim took, with no harassment from weather or midges. The faded blue sky domed above like a parachute, fleecy clouds caught in the seams, the sun at its peak. Behind us, the gulf of Glen Einich, from where we'd climbed, was steep and rimmed with rocky cliffs; before us, the walk to the summit was an easy rise.

When we got there, the views fell away on all sides in prodigal splendour. I could hear Shepherd, on her own midsummer day on Braeriach: '[T]here is nothing in all the sky but light. I can see to the ends of the earth and far up into the sky.' The southern edge of the mountain makes a dizzying drop into Coire Brochain, the exact spot where she lay down on her stomach to listen to the plunge of waterfalls and watch deer feeding in the corrie floor. In the warmth and hushing sounds, she fell asleep, only to wake with shock at the sight of the chasm right in front of her. Coming to full consciousness, she realised it was not so far down, but that momentary vision, untethered from memory or logic, had provided a shot of pure and terrifying sensation. 'I had looked into the abyss,' she wrote. We stopped to gaze as well, but had miles to go before we could sleep. Further south lay the deep fold of a burn coursing down through the Garbh Choire, and beyond that, the twin summits of Cairn Toul and Sgòr an Lochain Uaine. A high lochan sparkled between them and the glinting was picked up by the long ribbon of the River Dee threading south down the Lairig Ghru to the hill of Càrn a' Mhàim on the other bank. My eye curved all the way back up that ridge to the rounded bulk of Ben Macdui in the south-east, then Cairn Gorm just visible to the north-east, before dropping off the plateau to the lumpy moor. Directly north of us, the pyramid of Carn Eilrig blurred into the brown-green haze of the low hills and the forests of Glenmore and Rothiemurchus. Shepherd describes 'a thick place' at the hill's foot where she lost her path: it had once been the location of an illicit whisky still making 'a drop of the mountain dew'.

Further to the north-west, the forest gives way to the town of Aviemore. In her 1977 foreword, Shepherd wrote, 'Aviemore erupts and goes on erupting.' Back then, it was because of the skiing. What had been a quiet staging post grew to a village with the coming of the railways in the 1860s. Although pioneers had skied on the mountain since the late nineteenth century, the development really began in the 1950s, with local landowners and businesses seeing commercial opportunities, and climbing enthusiasts increasingly embracing skiing. Some had learnt it in Europe during Second World War service and nearly all proper mountain clothing and skis at the time were ex-army kit. When the ski road was built halfway up Cairn Gorm in 1960, and lifts and tows installed the following year, the eruption of Aviemore began. It also marked the early rumblings of conflict over exploitation versus protection of the mountain. This grew to another kind of eruption during the 1980s battle for Lurchers Gully over plans to significantly extend the ski infrasucture. Shepherd died in 1981, so did not witness that drawn-out and sometimes ugly dispute, but along with her blessing of those who ski, I think she would have been glad that the development was contained. Meanwhile, the volcanos grumble on. Aviemore continues to spill across the landscape and differing aspirations for the mountain and its surrounds persist. Less reliable snow and cheap flights to Europe have made the ski industry precarious, but other adventure sports flourish, from mountain biking to watersports to walking, all bringing 'uplift for . . . many hearts' but countless prints across the land.

Between Aviemore and where we stood on the summit of Braeriach, lies the hump of Creag Dhubh, Shepherd's preliminary walk to the hem of the Cairngorms. It is the beginning of a ridge rising along the western side of Glen Einich and extending upwards to Sgòran Dubh Beag, Sgòran Dubh Mòr and the glorious, craggy outcrop of Sgòr Gaoith – Peak of the Wind. Finally, looking back to the south-west, the plateau flows down towards Moine Mhor, the Great Moss, a wide, rumpled blanket of grass and bog. I don't think there is anywhere in the Cairngorms that offers a vision of all the range's forms and features, with the valleys and forests that spread around it, so well as this spot. Jim Crumley, whose poem 'Love is a Mountain' was in our wedding service, describes the Braeriach plateau as a place of miracles, 'as near to heaven on earth as makes no difference'. It's like lines from Shepherd's poem, 'The Hill':

> So hard it was that morn to tell
> If earth or heaven I saw

* * *

And then there are the days when it's not hard to tell the difference at all. Days when the plateau – indeed, the whole mountain – seems deflated and the weather dreich. One such was the first time I walked the Northern Corries, in 2011 with our sons, then aged twelve and ten. We were preparing for a family trek to Nepal's Annapurna Sanctuary that October and gradually extending our training. Shepherd had no children of her own, but enjoyed them, especially the siblings Grant and Sheila Roger, who stayed with her family regularly as they grew up. When she was a more experienced walker, she took children to the hills, even camping out overnight.

Our own walk started with a long trudge across the moor, treeless and dominated by brown and bog, under an indecisive sky. The route went through the Chalamain Gap, a narrow melt-water channel so choked with rocks there was no hope of a path and we had to scramble, one teetering step at a time over the coll in the middle and down the other side, till emerging onto the moor again. We puffed our slow way up the steepening slope to Creag an Leth-choin, or Lurcher's Crag, a prow of stone that rises from an eruption of rocks, almost as if nothing holds it all together. Balanced on the edge of the Lairig Ghru, opposite Braeriach, is the spot where Shepherd watched a plane flying below her through the chasm. By then we were harried by a cold wind blowing over the tops and had to don our hats and gloves, with waterproof jackets zipped up to our chins. Though high summer, it felt wintry. Luke asked if we could go home. We were going to, but via a mountain.

As we walked on over the stony ground, skirting bogs and scuffing our shoes on gravel, the sun struggled through the banks of cloud to touch the rivers in the western valley and the waters of Loch Etchachan to the east. Right around here was the spot my first Cairngorms photo was taken, nineteen years before. We paused for plentiful snacks or to take in a view or adjust our layers. We found rhythms of talking and silence, walking and rest. There were no heroic achievements or jaw-dropping sights; just the Cairngorms having an ordinary sort of day, dull and toilsome if you dwelt on your feet, offering surprise if you looked up for long enough.

I've had many more spectacular experiences up there, but I treasure that one the most. There is something about a long walk in mountains that opens us. At some point in the plodding, Sam, who guards his feelings, took my hand and said, 'I love you, Mummy.' Did I know then that it was the last moments of a little boy stepping into adolescence? That it was the last time he would walk holding his mother's hand?

* * *

By the August of 2020, Covid restrictions had lifted enough for us to drive round the northern sweep of the mountains and walk into them from the Aberdeenshire side. It's where Shepherd would have made most of her entries, travelling to Braemar by public transport or by catching a lift. I wish I knew what kind of rucksack she used and what she packed, as it's hard to imagine her lugging it all on the train and even more so, up the mountain, but she must have done. We took the well-worn track via Loch Etchachan to Ben Macdui. It's the same route Shepherd took on her first ascent into the heart of the Cairngorms in 1928, though the day she climbed they 'walked in a cloud so thick that when the man who was leading went ahead by so much as an arm's length, he vanished'. The effect only intensified. 'And now to the side of us there was a ghastlier white, spreading and swallowing even the grey-brown earth our minds had stood on. We had come to the snow.' That was summer.

Fortunately for us, and somewhat unusually, our day was like our earlier walk in June – warm, sunny and windless. We camped on the plateau overnight and, in the morning, woke above a frothing sea of cloud. A pure and perfect white, it lapped into the crevices a hundred feet below us and stretched out to cover the earth, shining in the risen sun. In Shepherd's words, at the same vision, 'It is like the morning of creation.' We sipped our tea and stared. At last, needing to move on, we headed up the trail. The plateau flowing up to Ben Macdui is littered with granite rocks, its gravelly ground broken by small patches of grasses and moss. Deer grass shoots up in wiry, orange tufts making the flatter stretches of ground faintly reminiscent to me of the Australian outback with its spinifex, or the arid lands of south-eastern Spain where many of the spaghetti westerns were shot. It's strange, how a terrain so often soaked in rain and mist or smothered in snow can, on a dry day, look like desert. When W.H. Murray encountered the deserts of the Middle East and north Africa during the Second World War, he saw an echo of the Cairngorms. 'There I discovered the same bold sweep of horizon and sky, the bare and boundless distance, the wind and desolation. The same simplicity.'

Ahead of us, a little bird trotted through the rocks in smart plumage of chestnut breast with matching black and white stripes on head and bib. The dotterel always looks quaintly incongruous up here, charming little creatures pootling across this savage landscape as if just nipping out to the shops. They seem unafraid of humans, often walking right up to them, perhaps leading to their name in Gaelic, *amadan-mòintich*, meaning 'fool of the moor'. Shepherd described an out-of-the way spot where she saw them 'by the score, running a little way, and pausing, and running on again, almost domestic in their simple movements. Yet in autumn this humble bird flies straight to Africa.' Members of the plover family, they return from the Atlas Mountains each spring to breed on the inhospitable high tops in Scotland and Norway. Gradually, we saw more and more of them appear, till a small flock took off and flew past us down the hill with their flutie, whistling cries. Meadow pipits followed in a tumbling dance down the mountain and the quiet air was rippled.

Near the top of Ben Macdui, where the ground is completely covered with rocks, the ruin of an old stone dwelling with a fireplace but no roof hunkers down in the rubble. It is where the Sappers – the Royal Engineers – lived for the autumn of 1846 conducting the Trigonometrical Survey of Scotland. The process involves calculating distances by triangulation and works best between points with clear, wide views, usually hilltops. Shepherd mentions the Sappers' hut, adding that 'an old man has told me how down in the valley they used to watch a light glow now from one summit, now another, as measurements were made and checked'. For people who know a landscape and its weather intimately, maps may not be necessary for navigation, but for most mountain-goers, including Shepherd, they are essential.

A hand-drawn map of the Cairngorms is, in fact, the only illustration that survived the first print run of *The Living Mountain* and is carried over into every subsequent edition. Shepherd knew that a map is not just an image of the land, but a story about it. The tales on contemporary Scottish maps go back thousands of years, as in the intriguing words *Standing Stones* that date to the Neolithic period, or walls from the Roman occupation. Maps tell us how land has been divided, owned and used, and to Shepherd, they were one of the many signs of human passage across it. 'Man's presence too is in the map and the compass that I carry, and in the names recorded in the map, ancient Gaelic names that show how old is man's association with scaur and corrie.'

As she recognises, one of a map's stories is about language. The place names in the Cairngorms reveal successive waves of settlement, culture and politics. Pre-dating the Gaelic, the oldest names come from the Picts, the tribes who stretched across northern Scotland from the late Iron Age to the Early Medieval period. Most of their language is lost now, but common words like Aber for 'river mouth' are believed to derive from them. Most of the place names, however, are Gaelic, reflecting its primacy here from late in the first millennium till well into the eighteenth century, at which point Scots and English increasingly dominated. Several names then became a blend of languages or an alteration of the original, as in 'Cairngorms' itself. The suppression of Gaelic language and culture after the Jacobite rebellions in the mid eighteenth century is one of the great tragedies of Scottish history, but there are strong moves to restore it, including on modern maps, where names are shifting back to pre-anglicised forms.

Of course, the oldest stories on the map are the contour lines, showing the rises and falls in the land and representing the work of rock, fire, water and wind over millions of years. This is what most fascinates me about maps: they are a script, a coded visual text on a flat page that depicts a living three-dimensional reality and a vast tract of time. I am still learning how to use map and compass. There are moments when it makes sense and others when it all dissolves again and I can't understand how this occult twisting of dial and calculating with numbers relates to what is around me. It is a layer of knowing the landscape that feels abstract and removed, that seems to hover several feet above it, captive in paper and plastic. But I know it isn't. Once I learn the meanings of all the symbols, lines, dots and colours, I can begin to 'read' this image of the landscape. And once I crack the code of the compass, I can hear how it guides me. As I learn this navigational language of the land, the tools will become the 'perfect hill companions', their identities merging with the landscape just as those of walker and mountain.

But we must be wary. Maps and their symbols only capture certain stories of the land, usually reflecting the motivations and perspective of the map-maker's group. A mining company's chart will be very different to that of an ecologist tracing bird migrations. Indeed, the mapping of Scotland began as a military exercise, another arm of the Hanoverian government's grasp across the Highlands after the battle of Culloden in 1746. Consider, also, the maps drawn and labelled by colonisers in contrast to those who were already there. The British possession of Australia and subsequent denial of indigenous land rights was based on the explorers' false map label *terra nullius*, meaning 'land belonging to no one'. By contrast, indigenous Australians have an ancient and highly complex system of mapping which is more about deep history, relationships and spirituality than technical measurements and ownership. They maintain an image of the land and their routes across it via song-lines, and record events on map paintings whose interpretation may only be clear to the initiated.

In her book *Position Doubtful: Mapping Landscapes and Memories*, Kim Mahood explores her relationship with the Tanami desert in central Australia through layers of maps. Some were made by early white colonisers, others by geologists charting millions of years, others by the Aboriginal people who live there, and still others by herself, as an artist and child of the region. 'To know the geography of a place,' she writes, 'is to know why we have always made stories in which our own human stuff is indivisible from the stones and creeks and hills and growing things.' To know by story. It is one of our distinctions from animals. We do not simply navigate our way across landscape by instinct and memory in search of food, shelter or a mate; we draw pictures, sing songs, dance patterns and tell stories about the place and what it means to us. *The Living Mountain* is, in that sense, a work of mapping as Shepherd charts her journey into the depths of a landscape and seeks to know it. 'Well,' she says, by the end, 'I have discovered my mountain.'

The hut on Ben Macdui reminds me of a very different ruin on a very different mountain, but with a strange resonance. In the north Indian hill-station of Mussoorie where I went to school, a once-grand white colonial house with pillars and a rounded portico is subsiding to grass and graffiti. It was the home of George Everest, the British Surveyor General of India from 1830 to 1843. He never saw or measured the world's highest mountain and did not want it named after him, but the decision of the Royal Geographical Society has stuck. The peak's height was first established in 1856, with remarkable accuracy, by Indian mathematician and mapper Radanath Sikdar. To the peoples who live around it, the mountain has many names, many aspects and many stories. The most common Tibetan name is Chomolungma, Mother Goddess of the World, while the most common in Nepal is Sagarmatha, a name whose origins and meanings are not clear-cut but include the Head of the Earth Touching Heaven.

Whatever the names, the stories, the measurements and the maps, '[B]ehind them,' Shepherd says, 'is the mountain itself, its substance, its strength, its structure, its weathers. It is fundamental to all that man does to it or on it.' Ultimately, to penetrate through all the layers of human construction 'to know it in itself' was her goal through *The Living Mountain*.

Above the Sappers' Bothy, the plateau is scattered with small stone shelters used in military training exercises during the Second World War, and most of them have afforded some level of protection to walkers caught in the mountain's notorious weather. The summit itself, which is little more than a lumpy dome, is marked by a cairn with a concrete pillar. A round direction indicator sitting on the top 'gathers the congregation of the hills into the hollow of one's hand,' wrote Shepherd. As we arrived, a runner bounded up to it and, hard on his heels, a family of five, the kids leaping and whooping across the stones as if they had caught the spirit of the meadow pipits. With the domestic bustle of the dotterel, their parents settled down to make porridge. Two young women in shorts puffed up next and posed for selfies, while a drift of other folk arrived, in a cheerful, chattering flow, talking about where they'd come from, where they'd camped, the names of the summits.

I am heartened by the variety of people you meet in the mountains. We'd seen climbers in bright colours inch their way up the precipitous cliffs, their voices carrying on the still air. On Beinn Mheadhoin, a sweating young man with tattoos had stopped to marvel with us at the weather, while beside Loch Etchachan, a very senior, silver-haired woman walking alone took a leisurely swim. Clambering up Derry Cairngorm, we'd met a family with a Scottish father, east Asian mother and two teenagers who had started at four a.m. to do their circuit, and that morning, a heron-like woman with long plaits had told us of her high campsite on a windless night, plagued by midges. In the hills, strangers will stop to talk and exchange notes, or at least nod and smile. There is a sense up here of both companionship and plenty of space. Shepherd commented on the same experience. 'One discovers that shopmen and railway clerks and guards and sawmillers may be experienced hillmen. Indeed, talking to all sorts of people met by chance upon the hill, I realise how indiscriminately the bug of mountain feyness attacks. There are addicts in all classes of this strange pleasure.'

As we stood at the top point of the Cairngorms that day,

the sun was high and brilliant, the views long. From Ben Macdui we looked back across the cloud-filled gulf of the Lairig Ghru to the ridge of Braeriach, where we had stood two months before, gazing this way. Beside it, the savage bite of the Garbh Choire and the twin peaks of Sgòr an Lochain Uaine and Cairn Toul. Everything was clear and sharp, as if our vision had suddenly come into focus. Beyond these forms, across the wide plain of low cloud, the summits of distant hills floated like mythical islands: Ben Nevis, Ben Lawers, Beinn a' Ghlo, Lochnagar, Creag Meagaidh, Aonach Mòr, the Grey Corries.

We had a brew of coffee and a chat with the porridge family, then set off south across the rock-tumbled terrain. Its lip yielded startling views down into Lochain Uaine, one of the four 'green lochs' of the Cairngorms. Not green that day, it was a deep, ringing indigo blue that softened to turquoise at the edges where the water was so clear we could see the steep sides sloping down into unfathomable depths. Above us, the sky vaulted in echoing blue, holding together the sharp ridge lines, the glowing hills, the distant horizon. The ocean of cloud had slipped away from the nearby chasms, and its retreating tide eddied like surf in the valleys. At my feet, grasses like threads of gold were tousled in the breeze and there was no sound but fleeting bird whistles and the rush of a burn. Perched on a rock high above the loch, I watched the sunlight spangling its surface and drew the world into me like breath. Writing of the mountain, Shepherd says, 'The mind cannot carry away all that it has to give, nor does it always believe possible what it has carried away.' No, indeed. The mind cannot even begin to receive it all, let alone retain or understand it, but in the act of trying, the self is enlarged. Beauty opens me; high mountain air stretches my lungs, far views flood my head, the whole wild presence of it expanding the whole of me till I become porous. It is not just the sacred space that is 'thin' but the person who sees it. Wonder pours into me and lifts me up, like a lantern, floating and filled with light. Perhaps it is what Shepherd meant when she said, '[O]ne walks the flesh transparent.'

IV

THE RECESSES

Life here is hard and astringent, but it seldom kills grace in the soul.

In *The Living Mountain*, Shepherd's chapter 'The Recesses' is the second, straight after 'The Plateau'. She begins by acknowledging her early lust for summits that meant she did not 'take time to explore the recesses'. The shift began when a friend took her to Coire an Lochain on Braeriach, where she was astonished that the exquisite tarn there was 'so open and yet so secret'. She goes on to describe places and experiences in the hidden parts of the Cairngorms that not only revealed the mountain's gifts but also unknown dimensions to her own inner life. Just as she seeks to cut through to the essence of the mountain's character, she discovers how it, in turn, pierces and illuminates her. It becomes a dynamic exchange. 'Something moves between me and it,' she writes. Then, as she comes to believe that she is as much a part of the mountain as the rock and soil, the water and weather, the plants and animals, she realises that it not only exposes but also changes her. 'Place and a mind may interpenetrate till the nature of both are altered.' It is another echo of Evelyn Underhill, who wrote, 'We know a thing only by uniting with it . . . by an interpenetration of it and ourselves. It gives itself to us, just in so far as we give ourselves to it.' And though the workings of this relationship remain mysterious, the only way for Shepherd to apprehend it is through words. 'I cannot tell what this movement is except by recounting it.'

And there is the paradox. She recognised both the fallibility of words – like maps – to summon the full reality of landscape and life, but the necessity – for her – of using them. In writing *The Living Mountain* she was, I suspect, first and foremost seeking to capture her experiences for herself. Perhaps that is another reason she did not push for publication originally. 'I have found what I set out to find,' she says in the last chapter. 'I set out on my journey in pure love.' By simply writing she ensured her discoveries would not be ephemeral and without significance. Art-making does that. It sharpens the attention and tunes the senses; it gives shape, reveals patterns, makes connections and meanings. It fends off forgetting.

But it is also fraught with struggle. As a keen reader, teacher of literature and reviewer, Shepherd knew good writing when she saw it, and also how difficult it is to pull off. Her correspondence is threaded with discussions about the challenges of rendering life in language. Writing to Neil Gunn of his work, she said, 'But that words should be able to convey this wordless thing – that is what amazes me. Yet they do. Something moving in the blood, yet fashioned in words. O my God! Words aren't meant for that. How by all that is unholy do you do it?' Her journey into one-ness of self and mountain was also a journey to fuse language with experience. But so often through her writing life, she felt she wasn't achieving her goal. 'Though I have now and then glimpsed something of that burning heart of life . . . always when I try to put these things into words they elude me. The result is slight and small.' How much I am grateful to her, my invisible companion, for such honesty; how deeply this resonates.

If the voice of her own inner critic wasn't bad enough, there were the voices of the outer ones. In the main, her work was praised in literary circles, but the highly successful Aberdeenshire author Lewis Grassic Gibbon was damning. He described her third novel, *A Pass in the Grampians*, as 'the dreich yammer of a culture's second childhood', going on to assert, 'This is a Scots religion and Scots people at three removes – gutted, castrated, and genteely vulgarised.' Later commentators have suggested it says more about his ego than her work and even question whether he actually read it. Her prior two Aberdeenshire novels preceded his and, in many minds, have greater depth and complexity. That 1933 review from such a prominent writer of her own patch must have wounded, but there is no record of Shepherd's reaction apart from a gracious contribution to the fund for his family after his untimely death at the age of thirty-four. It is clear that she cared deeply about the authenticity of her work, about the characters and the real communities they portrayed, about the technique of writing and the themes she explored. Speaking of fiction, she said, 'We want to know not only what happens but what significance it has.' She never wrote another novel. We don't know if it had anything to do with Gibbon, or because she'd lost courage or for other reasons entirely. Certainly, it would have been to do with the integrity of her work. 'I only write when I feel there's something that simply must be written,' she said. Apart from some articles and a short story, it was over ten years before she began the book that had to be written: *The Living Mountain*.

What, then, for the writer who has followed that inner urge, not in response to commercial demand or critical flattery, but because something must be written, only to have it rejected? She left no account of how it felt, but she seemed to bear it with the stoicism characteristic of Scots in general and herself in particular. Any emotional turmoil was hidden in the bottom drawer with the manuscript while she carried on with her teaching and her life in quiet dignity. But even though the primary act of writing *The Living Mountain* must have satisfied her need to record the encounter, ultimately she wanted to share it with others. It was more than a private diary; it was a 'tale of my traffic with a mountain'. A tale begs to be told. A tale seeks listeners. In the end – praise be – she found them.

I am one and because of her, I have found my way into the recesses of the Cairngorms and her work, discovering not only the interpenetration of place and mind, but also of two minds across time. Because of her writing, I am finding my own way to tell the tale, and because of her struggles, I am drawing strength in my own.

One of my toughest times recently was in the summer of 2019. I had agreed to help write the copy for The Cairngorm Story exhibition, a new visitor attraction at the ski centre base station while the funicular was out of commission. The previous October, a crack had been found in one of the concrete stanchions and the railway declared unsafe till extensive surveys and repairs could be done. If, indeed, they would be done. It would demand millions of the public purse and was bitterly opposed by some environmental groups. The event revealed not just the cracks, but the chasms, that divide the population over the funicular, with fierce and strongly expressed views on all sides. Even Shepherd had one. In 'The Recesses', describing the almost sacred inaccessibility of Loch Avon, way back in 1945, she said its meaning would be lost if 'jeeps find it out, or a funicular railway disfigures it'. At least the Cairngorm funicular, which opened in 2001, is on the other side of the mountain, where the slopes are already marked by the ski infrastructure, but that certainly doesn't mollify the critics. So, like a walker in thick mist, I blindly stepped off a cliff edge as I sought to reconcile the various histories and aspirations that cling to the Cairngorms, much like the tows, the weather stations and the crashed airplanes. As John Berger so famously put it, 'Never again will a single story be told as though it were the only one.'

'What story are you telling?' people demanded of me. What they meant was, *whose* story? The Cairngorms harbour many: an internationally significant but fragile ecology; a long cultural heritage; an exceptional terrain for walkers and climbers; one of Scotland's best ski centres launching the careers of multiple Olympians; moorland for sporting estates shooting deer and grouse; military training ground; sheep grazing pasture; inspiration for artists, photographers, musicians, dancers and writers; home to thousands of people in their glens and straths; the draw for nearly two million tourists a year; the linchpin of the local economy. Through the weeks of the exhibition project (and, indeed, my writer's residency, which was the same year but entirely unrelated) I heard many voices and views on what the ski centre and the National Park Authority should or shouldn't be doing. I came to feel that the Cairngorms' true, if dubious, distinction is how well they epitomise the tensions over land use in Scotland. Complex and intersecting, they stem – as most land conflicts do – from a long history. Shepherd recognised them in *The Living Mountain* foreword. 'Too many boots, too much commotion, but then how much uplift for how many hearts.'

Therein lies the crux of the problem for a national park: because it is a place of outstanding natural significance, it needs to be both protected and accessible for people to enjoy. The Cairngorm Story exhibition features John Muir, the Scottish immigrant to America who became the 'Father of National Parks'. He is much quoted, but in particular his belief that 'everybody needs beauty as well as bread, places to play in and pray in, where Nature may heal and cheer and give strength to body and soul alike'. Covid has not only demonstrated the truth of this, but also the unequal access we have to such places. It's also clear that if too many people go to them with 'too much commotion', nature suffers. A park's attempts to strike the right balance are never going to satisfy everyone – and perhaps not anyone – and it is false to characterise people as falling into two clear-cut opposing factions with ecology on one side and recreation – or economics – on the other. There are, for example, skiers pushing for more infrastructure on the mountain who know and love the nature of the Cairngorms deeply, and the same is true of some wealthy landowners and their gamekeepers. Conversely, some of the most expert naturalists are dependent on high tourist footfall for their livelihoods as guides, and they fly clients around the world for wildlife or mountaineering holidays, clocking up enormous carbon cost. The more I learned, the more complicated – and stressful – it became.

The pressure was multiplied by the fact that I live here, and friends, neighbours and colleagues all have a view – indeed, several views. Three locals, four opinions. 'I heartily disapprove of what has happened to Cairngorm in my lifetime and with the performance of the national park,' said one. 'Obsessed by tourism when it should be obsessed by caring for the phenomenal landscape.' He refused to have anything to do with the exhibition. In my other ear, a local stalwart gave his solution. 'What the national park needs to do is get their heads out of the capercaillies' arses and pay attention to the skiing. That's what this place is about.' Whether the park authority would take heed or not, I could not say, but what I did know was that the exhibition needed to be mounted in record time and, as mere copywriter, I felt tangled in the straw of all these different stories and asked to weave them overnight into a single strand of gold. The anxiety of it, added to my other work, personal challenges and the usual domestic juggle meant life had become overwhelming. Stress felt like a vice tightening around me and I couldn't get a single thing right. Not only was I forgetting, losing or making a mess of things, but I could barely put two words together. Rejections for my unpublished novel compounded the fear and self-doubt, till all my writing, whether exhibition copy or a full-length book, felt 'slight and small'.

I knew I needed to step away and take stock. I knew I needed a mountain. The Gaelic name for the one I chose is Sgòr an Lochain Uaine – the Peak of the Small Green Loch – for it rises above a corrie that cups a dark pool, so high it is hidden until you are beside or above it. I first learned about the loch from *The Living Mountain* where Shepherd says it 'has the sharpest beauty . . . a stark splendour of line etched and impeccable'. The summit above also carries an English name: The Angel's Peak. That name, the loch, the photos, and its position deep in the Cairngorms, had been drawing me for a long time. Some day, I had promised myself, I would go.

In a serendipitous gift, the diaries and the weather were both clear the first weekend in July, and suddenly that day was here. We started gathering our camping kit, borrowing and buying to fill the gaps, and plotting the route. Extremely fit walkers can get up Angel's Peak and back from Speyside in a long summer's day, throwing in the neighbouring Munros of Cairn Toul and Braeriach for good measure, but I wasn't one of them. Nor did I want to be. As Shepherd put it, 'Circus walkers will plant flags on all six summits in a matter of fourteen hours. This may be fun, but is sterile.' Certainly not fun for me, and why tear round the hills as fast as possible, beating myself to a pulp in the process? What was the point? I wasn't bagging Munros or doing mountain marathons; I didn't need to win or prove anything. In fact, the opposite.

I needed to lose. Not my things or my composure, but all the illusions that kept creeping back and tying me up in knots. I needed to give up. Not on writing, but on the pushing and pressure – external and internal – the straining to achieve, the seductions of so-called success. I needed to walk into the mountains. Not to conquer them but to surrender, to find myself at the mercy of things greater than myself; to go to the rock that was higher than I.

At the start of 2019, I had decided to embrace my term as writer-in-residence for the park as a kind of pilgrimage. Certainly, I would be covering a lot of ground delivering the project, and that would prove enlightening, but more significantly, I knew I would be on a personal journey, discovering new thinking about this distinctive landscape and its people, new territory as a writer, and new learning – I hoped – about myself. John Muir approached his mountain exploration as pilgrimage, reportedly detesting the practice of 'hiking'. 'Do you know the origin of that word "saunter"?' he asked of Albert W. Palmer, who recounted his interaction with Muir in *The Mountain Trail and Its Message*. 'It's a beautiful word. Away back in the Middle Ages people used to go on pilgrimages to the Holy Land, and when people in the villages through which they passed asked where they were going, they would reply, "A la sainte terre," "To the Holy Land." And so they became known as sainte-terre-ers or saunterers. Now these mountains are our Holy Land, and we ought to saunter through them reverently, not "hike" through them.' In fact, there is no evidence for this etymology of the word, which Muir allegedly picked up from Thoreau, but his ethos remains clear. For him, being in the natural world was an act of worship. He was not animist, ascribing personhood or divinity to natural objects; he did not pray *to* the rocks, rivers and trees, but would 'join the trees in their hymns and prayers', declaring that a mountain day opens 'a thousand windows to show us God'.

Shepherd did not set out for the Cairngorms in an act of pilgrimage or worship. 'It was a journey always for fun,' she said, 'with no motive beyond that I wanted it.' Yet, over length of time and depth of encounter, she discovered it had become something much more. In her final paragraph, she likens her mountain experience to pilgrimage, speaking of the journey as 'itself part of the technique by which the god is sought'. It is an echo of what she says at the start, about gaining knowledge by 'a process of living'. And so I realised, in that summer of my discontent, that I needed a physical pilgrimage; a walk into Shepherd's 'secret place of ease'. Sometimes, it is only through moving the body that we shift the spirit.

* * *

Beside the Whitewell croft at the end of the road, we rope up Sileas, our golden retriever, and shoulder our packs. I haven't done a camping trek in two years and it feels heavy. The afternoon sky is patchy sun and cloud as the trail takes us through the Caledonian forest of Rothiemurchus; it is deep with Scots pine and mixed with the many greens of silver birch, aspen and rowan. Blaeberry and heather crowd the woodland floor and the Allt Dhruidh burn chortles swift and shallow through the dappled light. I could lie down here and know peace.

As the trees thin and the path rises, we emerge onto rocky moor with the dark chasm of the Lairig Ghru up ahead, cloud massing on its tops. *Lairig* is Gaelic for 'pass', but the origins of *ghru* are debated. Nineteenth-century mapmakers arbitrarily changed Ghru to Ghruamach, meaning 'forbidding' or 'surly', but this substitution did not stick. Some say it is a version of Druidh, the name of the burn that runs down from the northern side, derived from the word for 'oozing'. Others say the name should be pronounced *lairig ruadh*, for 'red pass' because of the colour of the exposed granite. Whatever its name, this triangular cleft through the middle of the highest Cairngorms was once a route for cattle drovers and smugglers, but today we meet only walkers coming the opposite direction from Deeside and a mountain biker bombing down the track. With his long red hair and beard streaming from under his helmet he looks like an indomitable Gaul. I feel anything but, my heavy pack and boots making my gait clumsy and causing a sharp twang in the hip. In my Himalayan youth, I was a mountain goat; can I regain my hill feet as well as my head?

The rocky trail is lined with grasses, mosses, bog cotton and wildflowers, from buttercup yellow to the zingy purples of heather and vetch. Meadow pipits rise from the banks with their swift wing beat and bouncy flight, cheeping urgently, and we keep Sileas on her lead. Gradually, the path reveals the red shades of the Cairngorm granite: dusky roses, peaches and wines. The water spilling down from the mountain is so clear it makes the stream bed shine like polished copper. Higher up it disappears among the tumble of rocks, sometimes betraying its presence by a soft rushing sound, sometimes by reappearing.

Further in, the Lairig Ghru dims with mist, the steep scree giving way to the jagged cliffs of Lurcher's Crag to our left. When Shepherd stood at its top watching the plane making its way through the ravine, she observed that 'if mist had suddenly swept down, that passage between the crags would have been most perilous'. There are no planes this evening, but the mist deepens. It's nearly seven when we climb the high point of the pass and over the other side to the Pools of Dee, their surface metallic and disturbed, the clear water cold as frost. A bank of stones rises at the back of the second pool, and beyond it, a ghastly white wall of cloud, as if the world had vanished. Of the pools, Shepherd wrote, 'I can conceive of no good reason for trudging through the oppressive Lairig Ghru, except to see them.' They lie like mystical portals in this shadowed defile, giving no sign of their waters flowing in or out, or the secret of their purity. It is the March Burn that feeds them, dropping in a chatter from the eastern plateau above us before disappearing under the scree and appearing in silence in these pools; it is only further down the pass to the south that the burn reappears, by then as a tributary to the River Dee.

We pitch camp and cook in a blowing smirr, crawling early into our thermals and down sleeping bags, for there is nothing to look at but shrouded cliffs. The strangeness has made Sileas hyper-vigilant and she lies out for hours in the rain, staring around her and sending a warning bark at the slightest sound. There are deer and the guttural calls of grouse. Alistair eventually tugs her under the flap, but she remains restless. All night, my sleep is routed by the scant darkness, the tent rattling and the aching of my hips on the hard ground. I breathe wet dog and socks and wonder why the nature cure so often smells like this.

The next day we wait out the rain and it is mid-morning when we pick our way down the boulder fall, the glen unfurling below in the gathering sunshine. The view stretches out through the opening of the Lairig Ghru, beyond the buttress of Devil's Point to the smoky hills south of the Dee. To the west, the twin summits of Cairn Toul and Angel's Peak are still wreathed in cloud, challenging me to reach them. Tucked between them and Braeriach to our right is a deep glacial cutting, what Shepherd called 'one of the most secret places of the range, the inner recess of the great Garbh Choire'. It's where we are headed now. We ford the burn and strike out across bog. Small green frogs leap in front of us and the way is dotted with flowers, delicate and lovely in this wind-battered place. Tiny orchids lift tiered petals on slender stems, their purple patterns like embroidery on white silk. The peaks above us gradually clear and we can see the rim of the high bowl between them that holds An Lochain Uaine – The Green Lochan – and the waterfall that threads down from it, over black rock. But we can see no path.

We hop the stepping stones of Allt a' Garbh Choire, the main source of the Dee, flowing down from the Wells of Dee up on the Braeriach plateau, and push up the slope, finding a way among the stones, sometimes needing hands. Despite that, it's easier going than yesterday as I don't have a pack and my body is slowly remembering the footholds of youth. Cresting the rim, I go even faster, excited now, almost running across the boulder field until I see it. The lochan. The sharp-edged beauty Shepherd spoke of is muted by cloud, all greens dissolved into grey, the surface roughened by wind. It looks hard and so, so cold. But I am not disappointed. It is here. It is real.

I had hoped to swim, this being midsummer after all, but the pool is forbidding and I am frail. I remind myself that I have not come to prove anything or pit myself against the elements, but to find a measure of healing. For now, it is enough to be here, to kneel down and drink, to simply 'be with the mountain as one visits a friend'.

Much of this journey is about relinquishing high ideals and befriending realities. About taking time in the recesses. They are the deep and sometimes hidden parts of the mountain, spaces of darkness and dripping water – like the long cut of the Lairig Ghru – that can be either a shelter or a tunnel of wind, shadowed or pierced by light.

We need also to dwell in our own inner recesses. To enter these places of mystery, the cloud of unknowing and the path of night, for they are places of deep formation, of learning who we are and what we truly need. 'Life is difficult,' wrote M. Scott Peck in the opening sentence of his classic work on psychological growth *The Road Less Travelled*. The inescapable, universal fact of suffering is a truth central to all the major religions and the foundational tenet of Buddhism. Mental disorder, Peck argues, arises not from this reality but from our efforts to avoid it. A walk into mountains might seem like an attempt to escape from life, but the truth of what we find here – the demands of the landscape and the depths of ourselves – sharpens our sense of reality. In Shepherd's engagement with the Cairngorms, she always sought to apprehend the true nature of things: '[T]he world, which is one reality, and the self, which is another reality,' and how 'it is the fusion of these two realities that keeps life from corruption'.

Struggle, adversity and pain are not just inevitable facts of life but necessary forces within it. In my childhood in Nepal, I saw many people with leprosy but was sobered to learn that their disfigurements were not a symptom of the disease. Instead, leprosy removes sensation, so the sufferer is not aware of burning or cutting and does not pull away. The problem is not pain but the inability to feel it. Our senses teach us what the world is made of and how we are to live. In turn, the world teaches us what *we* are made of. If there were no hitting up against the hard stuff, no challenge, we would not learn or grow. In the same way, all close relationships involve a kind of wrestling as well as embrace; both are essential to the love between people, between the mortal and the divine, between person and mountain.

But mountains do not just test our mettle and make us tough. What if they nurture us, too? Recesses are not always enclosed or dark. They can be places of surprise and revelation in the way they open out and hold far more than could be imagined, as with the great ampitheatre of the Garbh Choire, which keeps unfolding into ever more corries like balconies above the central stage. They each host their own small performance of light, weather, rock, growth, water and creatures, ever changing and full of the unexpected. Recesses can be places of rest and nourishment, of shield from the elements and pause for a picnic or a snooze or a quiet gazing at some small wonder. And they are a holy land, as Muir reminds us, drawing us higher up and further into the mountain's heart, as here in the bowl that holds An Lochain Uaine.

So next we will climb beyond the pool and up onto the plateau to the summit. Over our lunch of oatcakes and soup, we scan the north ridge of Angel's Peak through binoculars. It was our planned route, but we decide the steep scramble is unsafe for the dog. Sileas beats us on fitness, speed and agility, but not common sense, so we start up Cairn Toul instead, traversing above the lochan to a less technical climb. From there, it's still a hard, steep slog into the wind and my body's memory of youth fades.

But, right now, it doesn't matter. By the time we get to the top of Angel's Peak, the sun has conquered the sky and the world is falling away below us. Though the wind almost throws me off my feet, I am overjoyed because I am here. It is like Shepherd's lines in 'Poem VI' from *In the Cairngorms*:

> Of magical and lovely light . . . Illumining the
> width of land

And all the hills that are –
Peak after peak how clear they stand
Father and yet more far.

Stretching in every direction, the mountains are billowing round tents of stone, rising in waves and walls of granite, falling in cliffs and corries, basking in light. Snow clings in deep crevices; burns are seams of silver in the grey and green; cloud shadows glide like sea galleons and mythical beasts across the slopes. Right below us, An Lochan Uaine lies dark and fathomless.

I do not know if I will return to swim there, but I do know I am changed. In this walking I have been washed by rain, shot through with light, battered by wind and hung out to dry. The mountain has shaken me hard enough to make my bones rattle and my head break its locks; it has beaten me like a rug and cast the devils to the dust; it has burned its image on the wall of my mind.

But, like Jacob wrestling with the Angel and wounded at the hip, I demand my blessing. As I walk the many hours home, I am remade. The mountain returns the pieces of me one by one in the ptarmigan's croak and the taste of a clear burn; it repairs me in the flowering of a wild azalea and the gaze of deer; it reveals my lost path in ancient rock, and lights my way in sun.

It restores my soul.

V.

WATER

*Water so clear cannot be imagined, but must
be seen. One must go back, and back again, to
look at it, for in the interval memory refuses to
recreate its brightness.*

Shepherd rose in the half-dark of a midsummer night from
her camp bed at the hillfarm cottage, on the Spey side of
the range. By four a.m., dawn was turning the sky green as
she and her companion started walking into the mountains.
Five hours later, they crossed Cairn Gorm and made their
way down the other side to Loch Avon, a jewel set deep in a
hidden gash of rock. It was her first time there. They ambled
in the July warmth to the upper end, arriving at noon when
the sunshine poured directly down on them and the water.
Clothes were shed and strewn across rocks. She waded,
naked and pale, into the luminous wet. Something else was
laid bare that day and something witnessed that marked her
forever.

I am beginning to understand what she saw. Like her, I am
drawn to water and compelled to get right in. But, unlike
her, I am daunted by cold. In the temperatures of South Asia
and Australia, swimming outdoors was second nature to me,
sometimes bracing but rarely an assault. When I moved to

Scotland nearly thirty years ago, I found it hard enough to stay warm on *terra firma* wearing multiple layers, let alone stripped down in the open water. I kept my clothes on outside and my swimsuit for laps in a pool.

But the day we moved to the Cairngorms in 2006 was the hottest that year, topping thirty degrees, and as soon as we had all the boxes in the house we went straight down to the nearby loch and cooled our feet. Thus began my thaw. Gradually, and with the help of a blubber-like wetsuit, I eased my way into the lochs and oceans of Scotland, till I found I could swim outdoors through the summer without it. At last, I got the feeling Shepherd describes of how 'the freshness of the water slides over the skin like shadow'. At last, it was feeling like home.

In recent years, there has been a growing trend here for 'wild swimming'. The older generation laughs. It was always just 'swimming' to them, or 'dookin' in Scots. Now, to do anything outdoors in Britain is called 'wild'. Perhaps it reflects how sedentary and indoors-bound we have become; perhaps it is to express the sense of adventure and freedom we crave in our centrally heated lives; perhaps it is simply to acknowledge how much we need to return to a more visceral relationship with the natural world. Whatever the reason, in Scotland, where we are flanked by the bitter North Sea and have lochs that freeze over every winter, it is not far off the truth. Some of my friends routinely break the ice to swim in black midwinter water; they are not just wild, they're of another world. But I might be starting to migrate to it. On New Year's Day 2021, I joined them for the first time, in my local loch, in a swimsuit. The water was two degrees and my skin so numb I didn't notice the ice cut on my thigh till I showered. I was also wearing Neoprene socks and gloves and a woolly hat, which make all the difference – to comfort levels, if not glamour. And that is one of the many things

I love about the outdoor swimming community here: it is about as far removed from *Baywatch* or Bondi Beach as you can get. People are all ages, levels of swimming competency, shapes and sizes, and it's not about body beautiful so much as body joy. And in that sense, it is wonderfully wild.

Shepherd is sparing in her use of the word 'wild' when writing about the Cairngorms, and she never used the word 'swimming'. She spoke of 'bathing'. In fact, her Loch Avon experience suggests she couldn't swim. Having waded waist-deep across a sand bank, she suddenly realised she was standing at the edge of a precipitous drop to the bottom of the loch. Its depth and clarity shocked her, and she returned to the shallows. 'I might have overbalanced and been drowned,' she said, but insisted the feeling was not of threat. Although it was 'one of the most defenceless moments' of her life, it electrified her because 'even fear became a rare exhilaration'. It is this capacity for excitement in the face of danger, this 'fey' sense, that characterised Shepherd; she was not fearless but said fear 'enlarged rather than constricted the spirit'.

I am not so good with fear. I confess to constriction. But I also recognise that different things frighten different people. On the one hand, I don't have phobias. I'm comfortable with flying, spiders, heights, lifts, travelling alone, public speaking. And I'm not afraid of death; not my own, anyway. But I am afraid of near-death, or the near-enough. The prospect of falling down a cliff, of being trapped under water, of crashing off a bike, does cramp the boldness in me. I've experienced mild versions of all these, and the panic and pain did not enlarge the spirit. Or did they? I didn't retreat entirely. I never got converted to rock climbing or shooting rapids, but I do still scramble up mountains, paddle rivers and ride bikes, on and off the road. I just don't do it very 'wildly'.

And neither did Shepherd. She also was no extreme sportswoman. She didn't dangle off ropes or lash herself into kayaks and there's certainly no reference to mountain biking. (It didn't exist in the 1940s.) She seems, in fact, to be quite like me in wanting as little encumbrance as possible between her body and the natural environment. Neither of us, it seems, are interested in all the kit and tackle of many outdoor pursuits. It just gets in the way. Like Shepherd, what I most enjoy is the immersive experience of simply being there. 'The whole sensitive skin is played upon,' she wrote, 'the whole body, braced, resistant, poised, relaxed, answers to the thrust of forces incomparably stronger than itself.' The whole self merged with the whole mountain.

And nowhere was Shepherd more immersed or unencumbered with kit than when she was bathing in the Cairngorms lochs. She stripped off. This is an astonishing feat, both in her time period and in those temperatures. In the summer of 1946, she took a young friend on her first trip into the Cairngorms, but, according to the girl's brother, 'Audrey returned horrified because Nan had insisted on bathing naked in a tarn.' Such self-exposure was vital to her, not out of any exhibitionism, for she was normally very private, but in her seeking after deep and direct engagement with life. In a talk about Burns, she said, 'To create, the creator must be in naked touch with experience. He must know his material in the raw, not canned in books or the experience of others.' The first time I skinny-dipped in Scotland was in Loch Dubh – one of the 'black lochs' – tucked away in the Monadhliaths, but my daring was simply because I'd forgotten my swimsuit. While I whooped and yelped in the freezing April water, feeling every intimate part of me go numb, our muddy dog, Sileas, leaped and yelped all over my dry clothes on the bank. The water was stinging cold, but afterwards, my whole body thrummed with a kind of radiant electricity, and I felt ridiculously happy. Maybe even a little bit wild. But on the day I decided to follow Shepherd into the waters of Loch Avon, I remembered to pack a change.

Today, the loch is more often spelled A'an, to better reflect the pronunciation, based on the Gaelic *abhainn*, meaning 'river'. Though the road goes a lot closer now, it is still a long walk to get there and still considered remote. It is also notorious for being brutally cold. Intending to take a circular route over Cairngorm and back through Strath Nethy, we parked near Loch Morlich and stuck out a thumb at the bottom of the ski road. As the cars whizzed past on that warm, bright day we wondered which one of us was most off-putting: the golden retriever, the scruffy man, or the woman in absurd sunglasses. It was early August, and I hadn't been able to find my sedate ones. Wonderfully, the vehicle that stopped was an orange VW Combi Van. I don't get excited about vehicles most of the time, but VW Combis and Beetles are an exception. They take me back to my childhood in Nepal where these charming creatures tootled around the winding cliff-top roads and got jammed in the streets of Kathmandu; colourful relics of the sixties and seventies, they had arrived in that mountain fastness after the epic, overland journeys made by hippies and missionaries alike. If anything was going to embrace the sweating hitchhikers, it would be one of these. The owners were young Dutch women who had herb pots on the dash (no, not those herbs) and an irrepressible enthusiasm for dogs and Scotland. As they dropped us at the top Cairngorm car park, I was reminded of how leaving space for the unplanned – not easy for a chronic planner like me – allows scope for the kindness of strangers.

The walk up Cairn Gorm was hot and even the normally exuberant Sileas could only plod. At the top, several people were milling about. My sweeping panorama shot was marred by a rotund older man in an orange t-shirt stood smack in the middle. But moments later his son and a small grandson came bounding across to him with shouts of glee, and I was rebuked. I do not own this mountain or any right to an unimpeded view, especially not on a sunny Saturday morning. When I lead writing workshops about nature, most people confess to wanting the outdoors to themselves, unsullied by the presence of others – or at least others outside their party. We seek an antidote to our crowded lives through the solace of natural beauty and the absence of social demands. It is understandable. I believe such quiet experiences are restorative, deepening both our inner and outer lives, and they were key to Shepherd's relationship with the mountain, which often grew in solitude. 'I've walked all day,' she wrote once, 'and seen no one.'

But I've also learned to welcome the presence of others, as she did. Without the leading of more experienced and knowledgeable guides, she would never have gone to the tops or discovered all she did, and over the years, she shared many of her Cairngorms journeys with companions, ultimately leading her own students and the children of friends. Like her, I am genuinely glad to see people drinking of the mountain's refreshing draught. She also did not presume that her long and quiet exploration or her relative proximity to the Cairngorms gave her superior rights. Some later critics have accused her of being a snob and patronising to the working class and agricultural communities she wrote about, but I think this is unfair and see evidence to the contrary. For example, she was generous in her help to the two teenage railway workers up from Manchester wanting to photograph golden eagles. 'I liked those boys. I hope they saw an eagle. Their informed enthusiasm – even if only half informed – was the right way in.'

The weather on the day of our walk was very similar to her first visit to Loch Avon on 'a cloudless day of early

July', but our approach was different. From Cairn Gorm, she headed east to drop down to The Saddle and walk up the loch from the bottom, while we went west along the stony ridge and then south-east down Coire Raibeirt. In Shepherd's time, the only way from the top end of the loch involved 'scrambling up one or other of the burns that tumble from the heights'. Fortunately for us, there are now several paths, testament to the efforts of the Cairngorm path builders and the growing popularity of exploring these inner reaches.

No one else was taking our route that day and I began to anticipate the isolation Shepherd had experienced. 'The inaccessibility of this loch is part of its power,' she wrote. 'Silence belongs to it.' Most people who have been there still speak of an almost sacred otherness; that whatever the weather, Loch Avon is challenging to reach and demanding to know. A dark, inhospitable queen in her towers of stone. From our height, we could see across the ravine to Beinn Mheadhoin, Loch Etchachan and the crags around it, but not down into Avon, and it seemed as hidden and secret as I'd hoped.

Beside us on the sloping plateau, water began to appear in the boggy ground in smears and slivers of puddle, gradually broadening to become a mesh of ponds that trickled into a downhill flow. It is called a bryophyte spring, where the mountain water rises through beds of moss, liverworts and peat, forming a spongy ecosystem rich with life. The angle got steeper and the trickle swelled and swifted into a strong burn, till it was rushing down through waterfalls and cascading pools. With the drop in altitude and the shelter from the exposed plateau, grasses and wildflowers grew around the stream: low clumps of sunshine yellow tormentil and tufts of harebell, their purple heads bobbing in the breeze.

Part way down the steep, steep path, we got our first

glimpse of the loch, a dark green triangle in the cleft of the ravine, so dark it was almost black. Reaching the shore, we could see up and down its mile-and-a-half length and the shifting patterns of sunlight and wind on its malachite surface. It looked deep and dangerous, but in our lather of sweat, so seductive. We took a trail towards the west end in the direction of the legendary Shelter Stone, 'the huge balanced boulder that has sheltered so many sleepers' even from before Shepherd's time, most adding their names in its book, including her. Our destination that day was not the Stone, but the curve of white beach at the top of the loch, broken only by a stream coiling down from the corrie and spilling into the shallows. It all looked so pristine and secluded, I contemplated naked bathing.

But as we approached it, a family of four emerged out of the boulder scree on the far side. Okay. No naked bathing, then. We tied Sileas up at a rock and peeled off our outer layers, aware of a few midges flitting into our faces. I'd decided to swim in my modest black underpants and bra and change into dry ones at the end, but now felt self-conscious in the presence of an audience. Too bad. Throwing decorum and my t-shirt to the wind, I trotted across the sand and into the water. To my surprise, it wasn't freezing. This end of the loch is shallow, and the long, sunny morning had warmed it. Though still a slap against hot skin, the water was more than bearable and quite quickly delightful. This was my first swim in a Cairngorms loch and felt like a rite of passage; a kind of baptism.

It was right here that Shepherd came to her edge. 'Then I looked down; and at my feet there opened a gulf of brightness so profound that the mind stopped.' Why? What was so intense about that experience that she could not speak of it with her companion and felt 'my spirit was as naked as my body'? I suggest it's because it was a near-death experience.

But a near-death of another kind. Both at the time and later, she insisted she had not been about to die because she trusted an inner instinct had prevented her from stepping too far. There was no panic or sense of peril. Nevertheless, she had found herself laid bare, in every sense, on the threshold of something both beautiful and terrifying, something potent both beyond and within her.

Paradoxically, in 'one of the most defenseless moments of my life', she was shocked 'to a heightened power of myself'. Somehow, that moment of total physical vulnerability, that glance into light, depth and danger so clear that the brain short-circuited, brought her face-to-face with a vitalising reality. The reality of death, the reality of place, the reality of her presence and – unexpectedly – of her own power. The near-death becomes the now-life. She expresses the same sense in her poem 'Summit of Corrie Etchachan':

> So may the mind achieve . . .
> a vast, dark and inscrutable sense
> Of its own terror, its own glory and power.

At Loch Avon, she waded back to safety, but the experience 'crystallised for ever for me some innermost inaccessibility'. In her poem 'Loch Avon', written in North Eastern Scots, she concludes, 'Ye'll haunt me noo for evermair.'

On the day we went, the light did not penetrate to the bottom, and I did not see what she did. For me, as a confident swimmer, that same edge was the moment of surrender to the loch, of relinquishing a foothold and striking out into the deep water, in exhilaration and trust. My body had long ago learned the language of water, the many ways to move and roll and float, to plumb its depths and ride its waves. It does not mean I am without respectful fear. I agree with Shepherd that 'the most appalling quality of water is its strength'.

But within its power, I too have found something of my own.

As long as I stayed in the water and looked down the loch, I could imagine the splendid isolation and silence she had experienced. But turning back to the shore, I saw Sileas running to and fro on her lead, yipping to join us, and the family of four drifting across the beach. And as I came out of the water with my sodden underwear and blue-white, goose-bumped skin, a wiry couple came striding down from Carn Etchachan. By now, the midges were massing, so just sitting on a sunny rock with knees up, waiting for privacy, was not an option. Nothing for it now but to wrap my tiny hand towel around my privates and wriggle through a change. Just at the moment of maximum exposure, madly hopping about swatting midges while trying to wrestle a sandy foot into twisted panties, six blokes appeared stomping down from the Shelter Stone.

It is so often the way. You can read the book, you can follow the footsteps, you can find the original place, but you cannot conjure the same magic. Nan Shepherd never mentioned any of this, but here at last, naked at lonely Loch Avon, I have an audience of twelve. Or three billion and twelve if you count the midges.

* * *

In her 'Water' chapter, Shepherd describes a midsummer day circling around the Braeriach plateau like a dog till finally settling into silence. She then realises that 'water is speaking'. Following the sound, she crosses a big hollow, 'a broad leaf veined with watercourses, that converge on the lip of the precipice to drop down in a cataract for 500 feet'. That current joins another one dropping from the Ben Macdui side of the range to become the Dee, the great river that flows for ninety miles to the North Sea at Aberdeen. Shepherd traces it back along the stony plateau to its almost hidden source, the Wells of Dee.

The first time I explore them is late September and the day is cold, but bright and still. It feels like the September day she was on Braeriach, when 'the air was keen and buoyant, with a brilliancy as of ice'. If it weren't for the map and Shepherd's description, I would not have seen the Wells or bothered to stop. It makes me wonder how often I walk past a thing of astonishment and fail to notice. Here is an unassuming depression in the ground: a ditch floored with gravel and clumps of moss. Then a tiny puddle appears, and another and another, but without a hint of flow. The shaded puddles are frozen, but so clear I don't realise till I touch them. It is the 'elemental transparency' that Shepherd describes. One patch of ice has the faintest outlines of ripples at its edge and vertical 'needles' suspended within. Further along, there are the smallest signs of water melted and moving, and where the sun strikes, the wet gravel is lustrous gold and coral. 'For attentive observation,' Shepherd instructed, 'the body must be still.' I take a few more steps then squat, waiting, every sense tuned in and tuned out. My camera battery has failed so I know I need to look closely and remember. The utter stillness of the mountain and my attention is met with the quietest, barely-there tinkle of water. The ice here is only a surface frosting at the edges, whitish and peppered with holes where it had frozen around tiny stones, but the thaw has now lifted. All along the meagre flow, mosses and liverworts plume, in every shade of green from acid to black, motionless above the water but wafting vividly beneath. When I plunge my fingers down into the wet, soft plush, it releases a cloud of sediment. But I can see no hint of animal life. Then a tiny insect appears, crawling over the moss, palest grey and the size of a seed, its legs finer than silk. And then I notice there are several, in the water as well as the mosses, and finally it dawns on me that there are dozens and dozens of them. This small faint trickle, in this high and empty place, is teeming with life.

I follow the seam of water across the plateau as it thickens and speeds, joined by more strands in this open, shallow curve, till they are woven together into a noisy rush plummeting over the lip of the Garbh Choire. From here, you can see the threads of further burns and waterfalls, glittering down the cliffs and corries, all drawn into the growing Dee as it flows south and away into the blue hills. The water seems to have energy and force of its own, that appalling strength Shepherd describes, but like her 'I have seen its birth' moments ago in nothing more than a flake of ice.

Water is the great shape-shifter. Shepherd observes that 'it does nothing, absolutely nothing, but be itself'. I would add that it does nothing *by* itself. Water exists and moves and has its being in relation to the forces around. Temperature changes it from ice to water to vapour; gravity pulls it down and gives it weight and power; movements of air lift, throw and drop it. And all these forces work together, none in isolation, so that water is never fixed, certainly not for long, but always, in some sense 'caught in the very act of becoming'. And water, in turn, is the life blood of the earth, influencing everything around it, by its presence or absence, its purity or pollution, its patterns of flow. 'All the mysteries are in its movement,' Shepherd wrote, acknowledging both the straightforward science that describes its behaviour, and the wonder beyond fathoming in the face of its power.

* * *

'The freezing of running water is another mystery,' she says in her next chapter, 'Frost and Snow'. She had dedicated an entire midwinter day wandering from one mountain burn to another to observe water in its capture to ice. Admitting that language may not adequately 'describe these delicate manifestations', she went on to offer word pictures of exquisite clarity and delight. Following her discoveries, I make my way up Allt Mor, 'the big stream' that runs from the ski slopes on Cairngorm down into the Glenmore Forest. It is early March, a time when the mountain can still be firmly in winter's grip. A stretch of water under a bridge in the woods looks fluid, until a certain angle reveals an intricate cross-hatching, like the frost patterns on a window. The whole decorated surface is thin as film and blends without border into the flow.

Higher up, more ice appears. It forms a shiny skin over rocks rising from the stream, tight as varnish and almost invisible. Climbers call it verglas and curse its slippery surface, offering the counter-intuitive advice to ford streams on stones just below the running water, as they will not be icy. Often, verglas sits like a cap on a rock, with its bottom edge fringed with baubles where the moving water has splashed and frozen. When the glaze has thawed a little, water slides under it in runnels like liquid tadpoles, swelling together and slithering away.

From the grasses, heathers and mossy boulders that overhang the burn, long crystals dangle in pendulous curtains, from cloudy to clear, smooth to knobbled. Some branches are caught in constant spray and 'harden to a tree of purest glass, like an ingenious toy'. Higher still, there is snow. Heaped in bridges and banks, it sometimes turns to ice on its way to the water, forming translucent towers and spires worthy of the wildest science fiction. On a rock loosely furred with ice, the water flow is caught and released in a rhythmic pulse that makes it looks like a breathing creature, a beating heart of stone on the living mountain.

'In short,' Shepherd wrote, 'there is no end to the lovely

things that frost and the running of water can create between them.' No, indeed. The only end is in the attention of the observer.

VI.

LIFE: PLANTS

I have wanted to come to the living things through the forces that create them, for the mountain is one and indivisible, and rock, soil, water and air are no more integral to it than what grows from the soil and breathes the air.

Nan Shepherd delighted in the growing things of the mountain with her whole body. She stopped to listen to trees and gazed on winter birches when 'the spun silk floss of their twigs seems to be created out of light'. Inhaling all the scents of flower and tree, she said, 'I draw life in,' and she carried sprigs of juniper for months 'breaking it afresh now and then to renew the spice'. Wild berries gave her delicious pleasure, like the golden cloudberry that 'melts against the tongue' and she loved walking barefoot where 'a flower caught by the stalk between the toes is a small enchantment'. In this total embrace, she came to understand that the plants were not only bound up in the life of the whole mountain, but also in her own. Hers was not a naïve joy, however. She wrote about both the 'tenacity of life' and the human threats to it, and *The Living Mountain* became for me a pathway into an ancient but disappearing world.

I'm cycling on a late spring day into a forest where she walked. The wind washing through the Scots pine trees sounds like ocean waves rushing up a beach and rocking a marooned ship, its masts creaking. Sunshine falls through the leaf cover, dappling the understorey and bringing a pink fire to the bark. Everywhere, new trees rise in a quiet army from the earth, from the tiniest bright green seedlings smaller than my thumb, ascending all the way through the strapping adolescents and elegant young adults of the forest family to the fully grown queens rising high as two-storey houses. Here and there stands an ancient giant, its weathered trunk a deep red and covered in plates of thick bark like the back of a prehistoric beast, its shaggy head filling the sky, its exposed roots 'twisted and intertwined like a cage of snakes', in Shepherd's image. These old pines have aged into a more curving and irregular shape, while the younger ones are upright Christmas trees. In among them, the birches are a blur of new green, rowans appear as slender surprises and junipers grow in their spiky clumps. Snapping them, I pick up that sharp scent Shepherd describes and push a twig into my pocket. Heather, moss, blaeberry bushes and grasses spread in thick mounds across the forest floor, while the clinging lichens on ground and tree give testimony to the clean air. Both broom and gorse are flaming with yellow, and the white wood anemones are perfect fallen stars scattered across the ground. Through everything, the earthy smells of new life. Walking the bike down to the riverbank, I hear the orchestra of birds warming up and the growing rush of water over rocks. Tree branches open to a sky of palest blue, scraps of cloud racing across it in the wind. Somewhere, off in the woods, the voice of a cuckoo. The first of the year.

I am in one of the few remaining fragments of the ancient

Caledonian pine forest that once covered much of Scotland. This one stretches most of the way up the Feshie, a shallow, braided river curving around the south and west corner of the Cairngorm massif. As well as rich growth in the floor of the glen, trees now extend part way up the slopes on both sides and are expanding their range every year. It is, literally and metaphorically, an uprising. Because, by the end of the Second World War, when Nan Shepherd was here, nearly all the trees were gone. 'Not much is left now of this great pine forest,' she wrote, describing the successive waves of felling around the Cairngorms through the wars. 'For a while the land will be scarred and the living things – the crested tits, the shy roe deer – will flee.' Writing specifically of Glen Feshie, naturalist Seton Gordon also mourned the devastation. 'The breath of the Second World War seared this lonely glen. Many of the old pines which had stood in their beauty for centuries were felled, lumber camps were established, roads were driven up the hillsides, and the salmon were dynamited in the river.'

One of the first things that struck me about my early hill walks in Scotland was the boundless stretches without trees. We could walk for miles – especially in the Highlands and Western Isles – get to a summit and scan the horizon in every direction, and see nothing but lumpy brown mounds rising from soggy brown bogs with nary a tree in sight. (Or if trees did appear, they were most often in the tightly packed and uniform rows of a timber plantation.) This empty landscape struck me as strange and, on a drizzly day – as so many of them were – ugly. What struck me as even stranger was how many people saw it as normal. Even beautiful. Time, experience and learning have changed me. I have discovered that peat bogs are not only natural, but rich with life and vital treasure-houses, storing more carbon than the equivalent space in forest. As I have understood bogs better and spent more time around them, noticing their network of shining pools, their delicate flowers and deep-dark smell, I have opened to their beauty. And as for the treeless hills, I do appreciate how, in certain lights, they glow with colour. Like Shepherd, I delight in the shifting from greens to blues to fiery reds. And, I grant you, without the clothing of forest, it is easier to see views, and the naked shapes of the mountains are more distinct: the sheer cliffs, the curves and billows, the jagged ridges. So yes, I do see their beauty. But more than ever, as my understanding grows, I see their barrenness.

The story of Scotland's plants goes back to the retreating of the ice cover, when there were none. In fact, no growing things at all. Shepherd writes that the alpine flora of the Cairngorms 'have outlived the Glacial period and are the only vegetable life in our country that is older than the Ice Age'. She credits her scientist friends with this information and says, '[T]hey are such jolly people, they wouldn't fib to me unnecessarily.' I'm sure she's right about her friends, but this passage is sometimes misunderstood. The botanists of today are equally jolly but insist no plants survived under the ice. During the Last Glacial Maximum, 28000–23000 BCE, patches of high ground further south, such as the Pennines, remained exposed and would have hosted plants. As the ice melted across Scotland, these Arctic species were the first to return, beginning with lichens, mosses and liverworts colonising the bare soil. Next came the grasses, sedges, rushes and ferns, developing heaths and grasslands. After that, the tree species: the dwarf birches and willows, followed by larger birches, hazel, pine and oak and gradually all the plants that make up the boreal forest.

Where there are plants, animals will come, first the microscopic and then those of scale and feather, till finally the beasts of fur, all in their own way shaping the landscape as they hunt, forage, tunnel, hoard, migrate, nest, brood and die. And so, at last, the people. They started coming about 9000 BCE from southern Britain, Ireland and Europe, which at the time was connected by land, venturing into these northern parts as summertime hunter gatherers and retreating each winter. Some of these early Stone Age nomads camped on the shores of the Spey near my home, leaving fragments of hand-worked flints when they moved on. Migrants, like me, they were already starting to shape the land, and over the millennia, began to settle, creating villages and farms. Some of my neighbours will be descended from them. As several roots of my family tree grow from Scotland, I might be too.

Five thousand years ago, the woods had reached their peak. The extent and nature of the forest is not known for certain but could have covered as much as eighty per cent of the land, including the now denuded islands of Shetland and the Western Isles, and spread right up the slopes of the hills. There, rather than an abrupt tree-line, the forest gradually shifted to low-growing, hardier species called montane scrub which, in turn, gave way on the summits to resilient alpine plants, what Shepherd calls 'the toughs of the mountain tops with their angelic inflorescence and the devil in their roots'. The ancient woods – that included clearings and different habitats, such as small patches of moorland – were home to aurochs, wild horses, boars, lynx, brown bears, wolves and elk. By then, trees and people had grown in number together for a thousand years, but from 3000 BCE, the balance tipped. Today, that original forest survives only in small pockets and those animals are all gone. Natural cycles of changing climate and soils have been a factor in some of the loss, but by far the greatest part has been human impact.

Shepherd was keenly aware of it and her chapter 'Man' begins with recounting all the signs of 'his presence' across the mountains, for good and ill. People often think of the

Cairngorms as wilderness. A high and remote space where nature reigns supreme, unfettered by our interference. In reality, over these thousands of years, people have moved across and used every facet of this range, shaping it as profoundly as the fire and ice. Our activity may not move mountains on so dramatic a scale as geological forces, but it does mark them and shape their destiny. The actions of people here have so altered the ecosystems that multiple species are extinct or threatened and the result affects the waters, winds, soils and growing things all the way down to the seas and up to the skies. What happens in mountains never stays in mountains. Shepherd understood these forces. 'Man's touch is on the beast creation too. He has driven the snow bunting from its nesting-sites, banished the capercailzie and reintroduced it from abroad. He has protected the grouse and all but destroyed the peregrine.'

* * *

The earliest peoples of Scotland used trees for fire and shelter and, as they settled, began clearing to grow crops and graze animals. The gradual decline in woodland continued until only half remained by 400 CE. Home to outlaws and feared animals, forests were cut back and burned to limit such threats, and felling accelerated as wood became an increasingly vital resource for construction, ship-building and fuel. Added to that, wars always exacted a high price in trees, and natural regeneration could not keep up. In 1503, 'Good King James' IV passed a tree-planting act, mainly to shore up the dwindled resource for his growing navy, but by 1700, total tree cover was down to four per cent. Then, woodland became fashionable among Scottish lairds of the eighteenth century and estates ramped up their cultivation, importing plants from around the world, while forestry also became a highly profitable enterprise, feeding the roaring furnaces of the industrial revolution.

But consumption always far outstripped re-growth and when the Napoleonic Wars brought high demand for wood and wool, the forests were ravished again and new seedlings eaten up by large flocks of sheep. Once wool prices dropped and Queen Victoria accelerated the fashion for Highland sporting estates, sheep were sidelined in favour of artificially high numbers of deer and red grouse, both inhibiting forest regeneration. By the First World War, not enough trees had re-grown to meet the rapacious demands of a new war, and the British government, realising its vulnerability, established the Forestry Commission in 1919. In an ironic reversal of the forces that had pushed them to emigrate a century before, Canadians and Newfoundlanders were brought across to help work the depleted forests beside the Spey and up the surrounding glens. But any recovery was wiped out, yet again, during the Second World War. The once beautiful pine woods were reduced to mile after mile of stumps in churned-up earth. In 1949, author Frank Fraser Darling wrote, 'Our land is so devastated that we might as well have been in a battlefield . . . see the wreck of Glenfeshie and Rothiemurchus that is no more.'

That was the landscape that Nan Shepherd walked through as she wrote *The Living Mountain*. In it, she wistfully recounts the shift in timber extraction from local woodcutters with horses and saws in small clearings to large-scale felling and floating of logs downriver, to the arrival of outside contractors with machinery and lorries and big sawmills. Ultimately, the forest suffered. 'In the glens that run up into the mountain, there are still a few of the very old firs that may have been the original Caledonian forest,' she said. Some of those trees – often called 'granny pines'

– still stand, but by themselves they could never restore the woodland because any new seedlings were quickly grazed. This is especially true of the lower-lying montane scrub, which has almost entirely disappeared in Scotland. As sheep numbers have steadily dropped since the late nineteenth century, being so unprofitable, in the Highlands now it is mainly deer that are the problem.

Peddling further up Glen Feshie, I come to an old stone chimney breast standing alone in lumpy grass. It is the remaining relic of the rustic dining hall of the Duchess of Bedford, who built an entire hamlet here of thatch-roofed huts in the 1830s for holiday shooting parties. Her aristocratic guests joined her in this bucolic make-believe, stalking on the hills by day and carousing in the hall by night. One of her guests, also believed to be her lover for several years, was the celebrated Victorian painter Edwin Landseer, who decorated this chimney breast with a fresco of deer, now faded away. He is more famous for the picture 'Monarch of the Glen', showing a regal stag looking out from a forbidding mountain landscape. It became the title of the long-running and highly popular Scottish TV programme about a Highland sporting estate that was filmed in this area, loosely based on a novel by Compton Mackenzie. Red deer are a Scottish icon, a tourist magnet and often voted the nation's favourite animal, but they are also one of its most divisive, competing for top spot – and for similar reasons – with the red grouse. Elegant and native, no one questions that red deer belong here. Shepherd was enchanted by them and her descriptions of 'this creature of air and light' are some of the most captivating in *The Living Mountain*. 'Their patterns against the sky are endless – a quiet frieze of doe and fawn and doe and fawn. Or a tossing forest of massed antlers . . . Its flight is fluid as a bird's.'

But what many people don't realise is the lie at the heart

of Landseer's seductive work. Far from lording it over his rightful kingdom, the real Scottish stag is struggling to survive in the harsh and exposed environment to which he has been exiled. Red deer do not belong solely on windswept moors, far less stony crags. They are mainly forest animals and their European cousins, who still live among trees, are much larger and stronger. For a range of complex reasons, but partly because our deer have lost their animal predators and resultant movement patterns, their numbers in Scotland are excessive and concentrated, creating too much browsing pressure. The relationship with their human predators and protectors brings further complexity. Where deer are fenced out of woodland (to protect what little remains), they are forced to live on the barren hills where there is limited food and almost no shelter. Little wonder, then, that they devour any fragment of growth they can find, and new seedlings don't survive. Such an arrangement makes them easy prey for the high-paying guests that patronise the sporting estates, but also means many die of starvation and exposure in the winter. On the other hand, some estates retain high numbers of deer for sport by feeding them through the winter and giving them access to woodland for shelter. This, however, threatens the trees.

Writing of the alpine flora on the top of the Cairngorms, Shepherd said, '[I]n the terrible blasting winds on the plateau one marvels that life can exist at all' – and it's true. On rocky ground with barely any soil, scoured by gales and completely frozen over for months on end, the soft mosses and delicate flowers are little short of a miracle. She concludes, '[N]owhere more than here is life proved invincible. Everything is against it, but it pays no heed.' Tragically, this is only partly true. Although individual plants and creatures do demonstrate an astonishing tenacity, the ecology of the Cairngorms overall is not invincible, but damaged and endangered.

Over the river from the ruins of the Duchess's hunting hamlet lie the headquarters for the Glen Feshie estate, in a cluster of traditional houses and large modern sheds. I visited them some years ago to meet Thomas MacDonell, a tall, quietly spoken man who grew up here, attended the same local schools as my sons and played for the Kincraig and Inverness shinty teams. He is Director of Conservation for Wildland Limited, the company set up by Scotland's biggest private landowner to manage his several estates, which include Glen Feshie. A striking landscape, encompassing the braided river system, pine forests and hills, the estate has been the setting for several films, including in one year when my teenage son worked as a porter, lugging cameras up the blasted heath to capture the exploits of both Rob Roy and Mary, Queen of Scots.

MacDonell made me a coffee from a scuffed table in the vehicle shed, led me to his adjoining office where a map of the estate dominated one wall, and told me about the day his thinking on land began to change. He had spent fifteen years as a fencing contractor, and in the early 1990s was erecting fences around woodland on a west coast estate. It was winter and bitterly cold with snow falling on the frozen earth. Before closing off the fence on the last day, he needed to flush out any deer and, entering the forest, saw several of them huddled in the lee of the trees. They were suffering from pneumonia and hunger, too weak to flee or even move. One by one, he had to gather them in his arms, carry them out into the wind and lay them on the snow. He knew they would die.

'They looked like refugees. It was one of the saddest things I've ever done.'

There began for MacDonell a long journey of probing and learning as he peeled back the layers of tradition and received wisdom around Highland land management and began to question the orthodoxies. By the end of the decade, he was working for Glen Feshie under previous owners whose interests were purely field sports and were frustrated by new legal restrictions on deer numbers. The estate became the focus of a high-profile government deer reduction programme, and since Glen Feshie's application for further fencing had been refused, the only route was culling. The TV footage of mass shooting, supported by helicopters, was controversial, but highlighted the scale of the challenge.

Recognition of the deer problem is not new. In an address to the Alpine Club in December 1945, F.S. Smythe observed, 'These remnants of the vaster Caledonian forest have suffered severely during the war, while selfsown seedlings, unless fenced in, never have a chance to mature owing to the deer which now roam the hills in herds greater than ever before.' Challenged by his own experiences and the passionate arguments of conservationist Dick Balharry, MacDonell removed the existing fences. Not only do they deny food and shelter to deer, but they endanger other wildlife and block their vital movement corridors.

Gradually, with the combined forces of the Deer Commission demands, official environmental designations, new ownership and MacDonell's evolving vision, Glen Feshie shifted away from the classic field sporting model to a diversified approach with nature regeneration at its heart. Ironically – and controversially – this demanded ongoing high levels of deer culling, at least until balance had been restored. Before they began, there were forty deer per square kilometre, and while ten or more trees blew down every year, no new ones were growing. 'I could see the end coming,' said MacDonell. Based on his research, from 2000 to 2004, Glen Feshie culled 1,000 to 1,500 deer every year, the carcasses sold to game dealers. It stirred outrage from some nearby estates whose own deer numbers – perceived to be vital for sporting reputation and resale value – were threatened. It also evoked horror to many in the community who saw only mass slaughter and a blow to the local economy. Some claimed that gamekeepers on the estate were shooting with tears pouring down their cheeks in distress for the beasts and anxiety at the undermining of their own livelihood. MacDonell said there were pubs that went silent when he walked in and childhood friends who no longer spoke to him. 'But I know how it feels to have your profession criticised,' he said. 'I understand the gamekeepers.'

The keeper in Scotland is as controversial a creature as the deer, and their portrayal ranges from Queen Victoria's much-loved and real-life Mr Brown to the fictional Duror, the embodiment of evil in Robin Jenkins's novel *The Cone Gatherers*. They are often the focus of rage when photos emerge of culled mountain hare (a legal practice) or poisoned birds of prey (illegal). Nan Shepherd's view was nuanced. On the one hand, she was all too aware of the human threat to the Cairngorms' environment. 'He tends the red deer and exterminates the wild cat. He maintains, in fact, the economy of the red deer's life, and the red deer is at the heart of a human economy that covers this mountain mass and its surrounding glens. There are signs that this economy is cracking, and though the economy of the shooting estate is one for which I have little sympathy, I am aware that a turn of the wrist does not end it.' She understood that one of the mainstays of that economy was the hard-working mountain farmers, for whom she had great respect, but needed to supplement their meagre income with field sports. 'On the crofts and small hill-farms wrested from the heather and kept productive by unremitting labour, the margin between a living and a sub-living may be decided by the extra wage of ghillie or under-keeper. Without that wage, or its equivalent in some other guise, the hill croft might well revert to heather.'

Crofting is a landholding system unique to the Highlands and islands of Scotland, where crofters have a tenancy for agricultural or pastoral use that often includes access to common grazings. In the Clearances of the eighteenth and nineteenth centuries, landowners moved crofters off the land to make way for large sheep flocks and then for sporting purposes or plantations. For the most part, people either emigrated or were shifted to small and poor-quality plots – such as on coasts and hills – where it was impossible to be self-sufficient, a deliberate ploy ensuring they would be dependent on supplying labour to the landowner. Crofters' rights and provisions have improved significantly over the years, with many now buying the land, but it remains impossible to make a living purely from traditional crofting.

A few crofters remain in the Cairngorms (MacDonell is one), but there are many more keepers, stalkers and ghillies, and from what I observe in my community, they represent the same range of human virtues and follies as the rest of us. As Shepherd put it, '[L]ife up here is full of loves, hates, jealousies, tendernesses, loyalties and betrayals, like anywhere else, and a great deal of plain humdrum happiness.' Like farmers and shepherds, most of them have a long and deep relationship with the land and an extensive knowledge of its flora and fauna. Several were key figures in helping Nan Shepherd and other early wanderers – like the pre-eminent naturalists Seton Gordon and Adam Watson – discover the Cairngorms. Indeed, some of Scotland's most eloquent advocates for the environment once worked as stalkers, ghillies and keepers, including Dick Balharry, who was awarded an MBE and the Geddes Medal from the Royal Scottish Geographical Society, and Alistair McIntosh, Fellow of the Centre for Human Ecology at Glasgow University. Experienced field sports stewards have wide skills, not least keeping clients happy through long, cold stalks on the hill, which they often achieve by telling tales of the place, its people and wildlife. They are as much keepers of story as quarry. Inevitably, they will have their own private views on the rights and wrongs of managing a landscape for field sports, but they are not free to voice much apart from defence of the status quo, for they cannot bite the hand that feeds them nor betray their brothers. It seems unjust, to my mind, for gamekeepers to be constantly blamed for environmental crime, such as the very real problem of raptor persecution, when they are employees under orders. 'They are not servile,' Shepherd said, 'but avoid angering the laird.' Landowners, on the other hand, must be held to account and, more significantly, government policy needs to prioritise benefit to both nature and the wider public.

Glen Feshie, therefore, is in many respects a model estate forging a new way. But it takes time. After four years of culling, the estate got deer numbers down to the goal of one per square kilometre, but nothing changed. Not a single new tree. 'We had the stolen lives of 6,000 deer on our conscience,' said MacDonell. 'It would have been immoral to give up.' As still nothing changed for the next two years, however, he started to have serious doubts. The critics were almost howling in bitter triumph. See? All those animals killed, and it didn't work. But in the summer of 2006, suddenly, an abundance of seedlings burst through. 'It was as if someone had flicked a switch,' he said. 'It was uplifting, almost spiritual.' I remember that beautiful warm summer, as it was the one when we moved to the strath, though entirely oblivious at the time to the quiet revolution breaking through the earth of our new home.

Eighteen months before then, the estate had been bought by the current owner, Danish businessman Anders Holch Povlsen, but only after MacDonell had given him a full and frank explanation of the estate's trajectory. 'I believe in telling people the truth,' he said. Povlsen understood and supported this radical approach and since then, the return of the trees has not just been steady, but swift, filling out the forest floor and marching up slopes that have been bare since the wars. The Glen Feshie pine forest has now doubled since 2006, including the beginnings of the scarce montane scrub, with no need for planting. They still cull 500 deer a year and host field sports, though the only grouse shooting is walked-up rather than driven, as the latter requires burning of the moor and suppression of other species, damaging to both land and wildlife. As well as the sport, commercial forestry and filming, Wildland Limited is developing accommodation and distinctive nature-based activities that simultaneously respond to and shape a different tourist appetite. MacDonell sums it up as, 'Enjoy, don't destroy.' Nan Shepherd would cheer.

It's a transition that demands not just time, but a great deal of money. With the traditional sporting estates normally running at a loss, the Glen Feshie model costs even more, certainly in the short term. Billionaire Povlsen has the resource to fund it, but for this to become a widespread approach, a root and branch overhaul of national policies and subsidies is needed. Pun intended.

Late in 2020, the Royal Scottish Geographical Society awarded MacDonell an Honorary Fellowship 'in recognition of your invaluable contribution in playing a leading role in the delivery of a pioneering approach to land management, particularly with respect to rewilding through the culling of red deer'. He is grateful but knows this is just the beginning: it will take thirty years to secure the woodland, he predicts, but many more to restore the landscape to a fully balanced, thriving environment with its key elements in place. Crucial to this process is restoration on a large scale linking a range of habitats and providing wildlife corridors.

With this in mind, in 2017 Wildland Limited joined with three neighbouring landowners – Forest and Land Scotland, the Royal Society for the Protection of Birds and NatureScot – to form Cairngorms Connect, the UK's largest landscape restoration project, with a 200-year vision. Meanwhile, on its eastern border and flowing down the Dee side of the Cairngorms, a similar story of remarkable regeneration is underway on the Mar Lodge Estate. Owned by the National Trust for Scotland, it is another sign that a healed land is possible.

Both projects include people at their heart. 'The problem with environmental conservation,' MacDonell says, 'is that people don't yet see their place in it.' He hails from a large extended family in the area, many of whom are land-based workers. His late uncle, Donnie Ross senior, was a shepherd, crofter and giant of the community whose views on land use, frequently expressed in the local paper, were diametrically opposed to MacDonell's. But despite fierce disagreement, the two men respected each other, acknowledging that both loved the land deeply, worked hard for it and cared about the people it sustains.

It is a much-needed dialogue, as conservation narratives often cast humans as the conquering, colonising enemy and nature as better off without us. They sometimes fail to see what Shepherd did: that we are an intrinsic part of it. And here is the profound paradox. Human beings are natural. We are not aliens or machines or invasive species from somewhere else – even if we sometimes behave like it. We are of the Earth. We belong here as much as the eagle and the wild orchid, our migrations and use of resource are driven by instinct like those of the arctic tern and the fungi, our bodies and communities are as beautiful, complex and precious as those of the honey bee and the deep forests. And just like theirs, our existence is bound up with the fate of every other part and particle of the world. Our challenge is to live this truth.

'I have walked out of the body and into the mountain,' Nan Shepherd wrote. 'I am a manifestation of its total life.'

VII.

THE SENSES

Each of the senses is a way in to what the mountain has to give.

'It began in childhood,' Shepherd wrote of her passion for the Cairngorms, 'when the stormy violet of a gully on the back of Sgòran Dubh, at which I used to gaze from a shoulder of the Monadhliaths, haunted my dreams.'

Looking down my street, you can see that ridge of the Cairngorms, and its changing colours and moods, are the backdrop of our lives. Soon after we moved here, I said to my neighbour that I hoped one day to walk along the tops of all those hills, and I was amazed when he smiled and said he'd done it, many times. 'What's that one?' I asked, pointing to a particular curving ridge at the back, rising like the tip of a wave above the flowing hills. 'That's the spur of Coire Ruadh,' he said. The graceful parabola is the only part of Braeriach visible from here, and every day it draws my eye, burnished to rust in the evening sun or angelic white with snow. In the busyness of raising a young family, of work and other commitments, it has taken me a long time to get along the tops of these hills, but the Red Corrie was like Shepherd's gully, ever waiting, tugging on me, haunting my dreams.

As with her, it is often the sense of sight that first draws mountain lovers into their thrall. We see them in pictures or on the horizon and feel a yearning. In a letter to a friend, Shepherd wrote about the effect of that same gully that she could see from the family holiday house in Kingussie: '[T]hat great gashed cleft above Glen Feshie, which I watched, year after year, filled with depths of a blue that made my heart turn over . . . And I dreamed my way into the Cairngorms thro' it.' We are reeled in, as if the mountain, in turn, has us in its sights and sends that shot of love. 'Something moves between me and it.' But just like any falling in love, invariably, we discover there is far more than meets the eye.

Looking at the Cairngorms from many angles, they appear to be little more than an overlapping, pillowy mass, and it is hard to imagine the cliffs and chasms within. It came as a shock to Shepherd, on her first climb up Ben Macdui from Deeside, to discover the interior of the mountain at Loch Etchachan with its wide loch in a rocky, steep-edged bowl. As any Cairngorms wanderer will testify, such inner cuttings are as much the character of the range as the rounded slopes and summits. Part of their fascination is that many of these extraordinary spaces are hidden until you are upon them. They are the recesses that so delighted Shepherd once she got past the peaks. The first one she gave time to explore is Coire an Lochain, under the brow of Braeriach. Meaning, simply, 'the corrie of the small loch', it is one of the many glacial cirques around the flanks of that hill, but the only one holding a body of water. It is a special place, not just because 'this rare loch' is the highest of its size in the UK, at just under a thousand metres, but because it is completely hidden until you are directly beside or above it. And there is no path.

It is early June and twenty-two degrees when we set out, Alistair and I walking in shorts and t-shirts. On days like this, I feel like a peeled prawn, my soft, pasty body finally out of its shell, finally in touch with the world. 'The whole

skin has this delightful sensitivity,' wrote Shepherd. 'It feels
the sun, it feels the wind running inside one's garment.' It
feels life. There is no wind as we start, but we carry the full
complement of weatherproof gear in our packs regardless.
High summer in the valley can turn to winter on the plateau
in minutes.

We leave the car beside the tumbledown dwellings of
Tullochgrue and Whitewell above Aviemore. These are the
crofts where Shepherd 'passed some of the happiest times
of my life', using them as a base when she walked on the
Spey side of the Cairngorms, sometimes camping in the
fields, other times staying inside. Returning regularly for
twenty-five years, she developed a deep affection for the
two branches of the Mackenzie family who worked the
neighbouring farms, among 'those who have instructed
me, and harboured me, and been my friends in my journey
into the mountain'. In her chapter 'Man', she gives a vivid
portrait of old Mrs Mackenzie – Big Mary – describing how
'for the few weeks of the year that we over-ran her cottage,
she was as full of glee as we were ourselves'. That cottage
was Whitewell, which is still 'this tin-can of a place', an old
white house butted by a stone byre with rusting red roof
and open views north and east across Rothiemurchus forest,
the moors and mountains. At the end of the public road,
it is still occupied and the field behind still dotted with
sheep. The nearby buildings of Tullochgrue, however, are in
sad ruins.

I look up at the dark beast of Braeriach, who has
summoned me, the remaining snow forming stripes on her
fur, the curves of her corries like jutting bones. One of those
holds our loch but gives no hint of it. What kind of creature
will she become when I am in her paws? The knowing of
map, description and gaze will dissolve into the knowing of
the body.

The trail leads through the Scots pine woods of Rothiemurchus, an enchanted forest, if ever there was one. Here, the varied greens of blaeberry bushes, mosses and pine needles are a cool opposite to the flame tones of the tree trunks and the new heather buds. Sunshine falls through the canopy in waterfalls of light, making everything glow and warming the sap to fragrance. It is like Shepherd's poem 'The Bush', where a tree caught in 'that pure ecstasy of light' has 'boughs of fire'. It ignites in me a deep joy that this beautiful old forest is recovering from the many wars against it.

We pass stretches of dark peat bog scattered with cotton-grass, called hare's-tail for its flossy, white tufts. Here, too, is scent and gladness. Peat is formed over thousands of years as plant matter slowly rots down in wet, acidic conditions, creating a fibrous, soil-like turf that can be several metres deep. For a long time, the importance of leaving it undisturbed was not recognised, and vast quantities were removed for fuel and garden compost, while bogs were drained, burned, built over, or aggressively planted for commercial timber. We now know that peatland is exceptionally precious. It is a powerful carbon store, regulates water flow and improves its quality, protects against wildfires, and is an important home for rare plants and animals. There is now increasing protection and restoration of this fragile ecosystem, that in turn supports such beauties as the golden plover, the bog sun jumper spider and the dainty, but carnivorous, sundew plant that feeds on insects. The dark, deep-down smell of peat holds all the potency of decay and the richness of life; what Shepherd called 'the good smell of earth'.

At the fringes of the forest, our route joins the Am Beanaidh, a clear stream tumbling down over boulders. That lovely, rushing sound always transports me to the mountain rivers of Nepal and particularly the Seti Khola – the White River – that runs along the valley floor below my childhood village, the constant *shhhh* of its rapids amplified to a distant roar by the cliffs. Stopping to listen to water over rocks reveals not just one, but a multitude of sounds; a subtly changing music with bass tones, melody, harmony lines and percussion. Writing of the water on the mountain, Shepherd observed, '[T]o a listening ear the sound disintegrates into many different notes – the slow slap of a loch, the high clear trill of a rivulet, the roar of spate. On one short stretch of burn the ear may distinguish a dozen different notes at once.'

Am Beanaidh runs north out of Loch Einich, down the valley carved by the former Glenmore glacier; at the mouth of the glen, trees line the burn and even grow in the middle of it, appearing to rise directly out of rock. An old alder on the bank is split open and listing dramatically to one side, but deep in its wounded trunk, blaeberries grow in a bushy cascade. I think of a giant dead birch in the forest near my house, black and damp, its bark like plates of crumbling armour from an archaeological dig. But it is covered in mosses, fungi and lichen, crawling with insects, visited by birds and adorned with wildflowers; and rising right out of its top, fifteen feet up, is a young Scots pine seedling. It is often said that there is more life in a dead tree than a living one. Life grows out of death and, often, as with peat, the dying itself is necessary for new life, the very ground of its being.

Higher up, where the first, gentle slopes of the glen begin to steepen, the trees give way to masses of broom and gorse in flaming yellow, and a bit further on, we are in the familiar open moorland landscape of low, patchy heather with the occasional, rare Scots pine. There is no trail to Loch Coire an Lochain, and this route from below is rarely used. It's the one Shepherd took in the company of her 'rabid naturalist' friend who 'had business with every root, stalk and flower'. He was J. Grant Roger, the older brother of Sheila Roger, the siblings who became the closest thing to Shepherd's own children. Roger grew up to become a botanist and one of the founding members of the Nature Conservancy, an organisation Shepherd mentions in the foreword to her book. With responsibility for Scotland's North East, including his beloved Cairngorms, Roger's greatest passion was mountain flowers.

Without stepping stones, we have to peel off socks and shoes to ford the Beanaidh Bheag burn dropping down from Braeriach and, even on a warm June day, it is bracing. This was how Shepherd often ended up walking barefoot. 'It begins with a burn that must be forded: once my shoes are off, I am loth to put them on again.' My white, shelled feet summon Pablo Neruda's haunting poem 'To the Foot from its Child' in which the foot is imprisoned in a shoe for its whole life and always working so hard that it 'hardly had time / to be naked in love or in sleep'. If we are not mindful, our walking can abuse the feet in the same way, condemning them to boots and hard labour without pause to breathe. Shepherd allowed her whole body and all of her senses to experience the mountain and, in so doing, opened ever more pathways of discovery and pleasure.

Our discovery now lies across a kilometre of tussocky moor, which would have been a muddy travail were it not for the recent dry spell, which has hardened the ground and bleached the grasses. Even the mosses are pale and crackly as straw. We pass a row of rickety wooden structures made of a few fence palings, originally for driven grouse shooting, though now disused. A peat hag harbours the skeleton roots of an old Scots pine from millennia gone by, its bone-pale remains being the 'rossity reets' that Shepherd describes, the dried fir roots that the croft women dug from the moor for their fire.

Beyond, the slope steepens and becomes a spill of rocks

as we scramble up, sweating and breathless in the midday warmth. The hard grey of the granite is broken by small patches of trailing azalea, their dark green leaves and tiny pink flowers a startling union of resilience and delicacy in this harsh terrain. Shepherd said the mountain never quite gives away the 'secret of growth' but that we find hints of it in such astonishing plants as these: '[T]he miniature azalea that grows splayed against the mountain for protection, and lures the rare insects by its rosy hue.' And the mountain never quite gives away the secret of beauty, either: why we are delighted by this flower that has no obvious use to us; why we are drawn up a hill. For it's not easy to get here. Even as the ground levels and the corrie wall towers before us, there is no sign of water, and we must trudge across a seemingly endless boulder field. 'A tough bit of going,' Shepherd warned.

Finally – suddenly – as if by magic, the loch appears. And it does have the impossibility of magic about it: between the foreground rim of faded boulders and the backdrop of curving cliffs, lies a perfect, dark pool. The lightest of breezes dimples its skin and catches sunlight in a million sparks. The sound of rushing water carries from the precipice above and I can see it skimming down over the scree and disappearing under banks of snow, but its fall into the loch is hidden, the surface unbroken. 'Climb as often as you will,' Shepherd said, 'Loch Coire an Lochain remains incredible.'

It was standing here that she made her revelatory experiments with perception, moving her gaze slowly from one edge of the loch to the other, turning around to see the expanse of the Spey valley and its hills to the north, and dropping her head to look upside down between her legs. 'The focal point is everywhere,' she found. 'Nothing has reference to me, the looker. This is how the earth must see itself.' Much of her approach to exploring the mountain was one of quiet disruption. Not to be rebellious or to upend anyone else's way of walking, but as an inevitable result of her seeking after its 'essential nature'. Increasingly, she subverted the normal expectations of how to be a mountaineer, shifting from the 'tang of height' to an ever-slower meandering in the depths; increasingly, she challenged herself to find new and more primal ways of experiencing the natural world, 'living in one sense at a time to live all the way through'; increasingly, she sought a new understanding of what is real and true.

In this last, her disruption involved a gradual shift in world view. Brought up in the Presbyterian Free Church, the psalms, hymns and poems she copied into her notebook as a teenager reflect a passionate and personal faith. But through adulthood she explored beyond it to learn from other philosophies and loosened her ties to institutional Christianity. She left no explicit account of this journey, though the ranging of her ideas is clear from her writing, reading and letters. There were several probable influences. For many at the time, the First World War had a shattering effect on belief in the goodness of God and the righteousness of believers who could orchestrate such violence; the death of her newly-married brother (and only sibling) from TB in 1917 was a fierce blow, as was her father's death in 1925; her intellectual inquiry through university and beyond, including friendships and dynamic correspondence with writers and philosophers, led her to consider radically different perspectives; and, by contrast, the church at the time could be narrow, didactic and censorious. Significantly, Aberdeen was a conservative place, and the combination of Victorian prudery, war deprivations, the depression and a puritanical streak in Scottish Presbyterianism would have fostered a culture at least reticent about, if not downright disapproving of, sensory pleasure. Shepherd was not hedonistic or self-indulgent – foregoing fashion and living an apparently celibate, simple, if comfortable, existence – but it is clear from her writing that she was sensuous, revelling in the natural world and wanting to respond to it, body and soul. Therefore, it seems, if her church's teaching granted ecstasy of soul alone, often at the subjugation of the body, she would quietly walk away.

The visit Shepherd describes to this loch was in September after equinoctial storms, and on that occasion she only dipped her fingers in the 'frost-cold' water. For us, on a warm June day with barely any wind, it is a chance to swim. I strip down to my underwear, don Neoprene booties and stand at the water's edge. In my reckless youth, I thought the only way to enter cold water was by hurtling in, full tilt, and getting immersed before the body had time to revolt. This usually meant the body revolted anyway and I was soon hurtling back out. Now, I take it slowly. It's never a good idea to court cold-water shock, and at 3,000 feet up in a remote corrie, it is a particularly bad idea. The life of the senses must include that rarest one of all, called 'common'.

By the time she was writing *The Living Mountain*, Shepherd had not been a churchgoer for over twenty years and had been exploring philosophies, of 'Eastern' and mystical roots, for even longer. Some of these were copied into her notebooks, including extracts from a translation of the Chinese text *Tao Te Ching* and *Gleanings in Buddha-Fields*. The latter was by the Greek-Irish-American writer Lafcadio Hearn, who adopted Japanese citizenship, Buddhism and the name Koizumi Yakumo. Shepherd also read the Irish 'Celtic Twilight' poet and theosophist George William Russell, who took the name Æon, representing the lifelong quest of man. The six poems of his that she transcribed all explore the 'religion of nature'. The only poet to whom she gave more space was Rabindranath Tagore, who wrote from a Hindu tradition but with a universalist vision. In all these works, the idea of the 'one-ness', or connectedness, of all things is a strong theme, and it is one that underlies *The Living Mountain*. Perhaps more significant than the copied quotes, is her long correspondence with Neil Gunn, revealing a deep, mutual probing into the meanings of existence and the substance of true experience.

It seems to me that Shepherd found in these evolving ideas a relationship with the physical world that her church heritage had failed to offer. For many and complex reasons, the Free Church Presbyterianism of her time – and of many Christian traditions then and still – separated and prioritised the spiritual over the material. The soul was paramount, and not only was the body inferior but potentially a threat to the soul's progress. It engendered the 'sins of the flesh' and could not be trusted. Thus, it could not be enjoyed and must be disciplined, denied and disguised. Even despised. By the same logic, heaven is the goal; and Earth at best a waiting room, at worst the 'City of Destruction' that John Bunyan's Pilgrim must escape.

* * *

I balance on a boulder at the edge of the loch, scan its surface and brace my body. Because the water has no peat or sediment, it is startlingly clear, the granite rocks below the surface luminous in shades of coral and turquoise. A few metres out, the water deepens to black, and twenty metres beyond, it meets the cliff under an overhang of snow. To enter this pool feels like breaking the wall to another dimension. For a few seconds as I wobble across the nearest submerged rock, the booties mute the cold, but then the water slices my ankles. All the hairs on my legs rise. I creep on, an inch at a time, the ice cold stealing up to my knees, my thighs, my waist. It is so cold it has flipped my nerve endings and feels like a burning across the skin. The hardest moment is surrendering my warm back to the freezing water, but once it is done, I lift my feet and push off into the great, ringing cold, yielding myself like an offering to the holy lake.

For this is holy. Everything about this place is knife sharp: the brilliance of sky, the curve of ridge, the gleam of sunlight on snow and loch, the hardness of granite and the bite of water. To encounter the tangible world in all its intensity is almost unbearable; it hurts the eyes, the coddled skin, the soft feet. But it pares you back and wakens you, in every cell of your being, and says, *This is real*. Shepherd's description is perfect. 'This plunge into the cold water of a mountain pool seems for a brief moment to disintegrate the very self; it is not to be borne: one is lost: stricken: annihilated. Then life pours back.'

It resonates with C.S. Lewis's *The Great Divorce*, where the plains of heaven have such substance it is too painful for the wraith-like visitors from the grey town. They can barely walk over the blades of grass that are hard as diamond, or lift an apple that is heavier than iron. 'Will you come with me to the mountains?' invites a resident of heaven. 'It will hurt at first, until your feet are hardened. Reality is harsh to the feet of shadows. But will you come?' And that is the paradox. The sacred is mystery and holiness and life intensified 'to the point of glory', but it is not a spiritual realm in denial of the material. Neither is it illusion or delusion. The sacred is reality most true. As Shepherd observes, it is not the 'leap out of the self', but a fully conscious presence within the embodied self. The transcendent made immanent.

After swimming in the searing cold for a few minutes, I retreat to a rock in the sun to ease my skin, and then – to my own surprise – I go back to the water. It seems too extraordinary an encounter to abandon so quickly. But I do not put my head under. I have learned from experience that doing that with a bare head can bring on such an assault that my core temperature plummets and my skull pounds for ages. There is a level of pain that enlivens experience, and a level that annihilates it. Out again, I strip off and rub down, and there is something wild and joyous about standing stark naked beside this high loch, trusting every vulnerable part of me to this demanding landscape. But it is easy to feel such freedom, as this place is so remote and difficult to reach that I am confident no one will appear. It is certainly far less travelled than Loch Avon. Nevertheless, it is always at moments like this that Alistair gives a wave and a cheery greeting to a supposed visitor heaving into view. There is no one, of course, but if someone had soldiered the hard yards to get here, they probably deserved some entertainment. Eating our packed lunch in the sunshine, our humble cheese sandwiches are a feast, and the bottle of pure loch water has turned to wine.

The truth about my body lies in the paradox of freedom and discipline. I believe the body is inherently good and made for pleasure. But if I live only for pleasure and indulge the desires of my flesh without regard for my fellow person and the Earth, I ultimately destroy others and our world. I even destroy my own capacity for pleasure and, ultimately, myself. So yes, the body must be disciplined. By training it and 'keying the senses', as Shepherd would say, I can get up into the mountains and receive more of what they have to offer. In the same way, to receive their bounty, I need to 'know' through my body and to trust and celebrate it. The beauty of the body is not in the eye of an external beholder but in what the body itself be-holds: in its Being and its Holding. The body, finely tuned to see, hear, smell, taste and touch, now *holds* the beauty of the Earth. And yet cannot possibly hold it, for it is too great to contain. As Shepherd says, 'If I had other senses, there are other things I should know . . . Yet, with what we have, what wealth!'

We walk over the outflow stream at the end of the loch, across a bank of snow and up the rocky western shoulder of the corrie. On the way up, a pair of ptarmigan appear among the scree in their summer plumage of mottled brown and grey. The male struts and poses on the rocks, giving the occasional warning croak, while the female treads quietly, slipping in and out of view. Pacing up the slope ahead of us, they occasionally speed up, but never fly, and when they venture across patches of snow, I wonder if they know – if they are capable of knowing – that they are no longer camouflaged against it, as they would be in their winter whites. With the change of the seasons, do they see themselves in a different way?

We are lucky to spot these elusive birds, lucky to be on this sun-drenched mountain, lucky to be healthy enough to walk here and to have our five senses. What of the bodies that are aged, or tired, or sick, or disabled? What does the fullness of life mean for them? Shepherd offered wisdom from her own time of physical limitation because of illness in her seventies. 'I can again just be. A cessation of doing in which one begins to know being.' Sometimes, the loss of something in our body enables gain in another part of ourselves, a focusing and heightening of what remains. She noted this when struggling to find her footing on a familiar trail on a very dark night. 'To be a blind man, I see, needs application.' So, I am deeply glad that there is ever more work to enable people with physical challenges to be in mountains. 'Body' is not just a word for an individual, but also for a group joined for a purpose. The body of the church, a body of people. No one has learned on their own to be in mountains, including the very athletic and those who take solo trips. We have all come here via guides, training, books, maps, paths and the presence of others. We are always companioned, even if not in time.

Below us, the loch shifts through the spectrum of blues from aquamarine to sapphire to midnight depending on the angle of our climb and the behaviour of cloud, shadows and wind. It is never the same. This is the loch Shepherd spoke of, that even when veiled by mist, 'the stones at the bottom are still intense and bright, as though the water itself held radiance'. To know the essence of anything is to recognise how it changes in relation to everything around, to capture it, as she says, 'in the very act of becoming'. The loch has no innate colour; it only has water and minerals that interact with air and light to create, in the eye of the viewer, an image. That image is different for me than for a ptarmigan or a deer, and different even from another person, who not only perceives colour in a different way, but looks on a loch with different meaning. To one it represents fear; to another a subject of scientific study; a third person may barely notice it at all, for their interests are elsewhere. For me, it is a place of inaccessible beauty to which I have been granted access; a holy of holies; a swim. If this variance of perspective is true of inanimate objects, how much more so of people, in all their glorious complexity. 'Such illusions,' said Shepherd, 'depending on how the eye is placed and used, drive home the truth that our habitual vision of things is not necessarily right: it is only one of an infinite number, and to glimpse an unfamiliar one, even for a moment, unmakes us, but steadies us again.'

And so we discover that we do not know all we think we know, and that humility, therefore, is the beginning of wisdom. But for all our limitation and subjectivity, the thing to be known is there, is real and holds an 'essential nature' beyond all interpretations of it. The loch exists, the mountain lives, the human being *is*.

After wandering Braeriach's rolling plateau, we walk back down the spine between Coire an Lochain and its eastern neighbour Coire Ruadh – the Red Corrie. I realise with a thrill that this is the ethereal curve of mountain that I have gazed at for fourteen years from my street, that has haunted my dreams. This is the imagined made real. And it is nothing like I imagined. Nothing ever is. Reality demands that we surrender the fantasy to take hold of what is true.

Mountain experiences never end on the mountain. There is always the long walk home. The knee-shattering down, down, down over hard rock; the boots plunging into holes hidden by growth or into sucking wells of mud; the slow, repetitive trudge all the way back. It can be tempting to try to get it over with. The day has peaked, and we want to fast forward to home, hot shower, dinner and bed. But the mountain carries on living and giving, if we care to notice. The tips of new growth on the heather are fire-poker red, and just as Shepherd testified, walking on it barefoot is soft and easy. Across the expanses of bog, small butterflies dizzy from plant to plant, while lizards and toads appear and disappear in flashes of slick, speckled backs. Half-hidden behind a rock is an exquisite wildflower I have never seen before with four white petals offset by four green sepals and a flurry of yellow stamens at its heart. Perfectly symmetrical, it is the blossom of the cloudberry, the sweet mountain bramble that looks like an orange raspberry in autumn and whose flavour, said Shepherd, could not be described but only experienced. 'One must find the berries, golden-ripe, to know their taste.'

We peel off socks and shoes for the last time to ford the Beanaidh Bheag and sit on the other side eating chocolate biscuits as our throbbing feet dry. The last two hours we fall into a weary quiet, no energy beyond the steady step, step, step. Our bodies are tired, but our heads brimming.

VIII.

LIFE: BIRDS, ANIMALS, INSECTS

*Imagination is haunted by the swiftness of
the creatures that live on the mountain.*

When Nan Shepherd wrote about the beings she
encountered in her Cairngorms wandering, she was
not interested in purely factual information. 'But why should
I make a list? It serves no purpose, and they are all in the
books.' Her own book had a different goal: to recount how
she came to know the mountain through a 'process of living'.
So, when she describes the birds and animals, it is not just
their characteristics that she notes – although she does so
vividly – but also the way they move and shape her. She tells
how watching swifts in their 'convolutions of delight' made
her laugh aloud with the 'same feeling of release as though I
had been dancing for a long time'.

It's a telling metaphor. She had obviously experienced the
loosing of inhibition that dancing brings – for those who
enjoy it. I am a dance lover, too, and it was one of my majors
at university. We learned about the kinaesthetic response:
how our bodies can *feel* something we are observing.
Shepherd did not use that term but she captured the idea
exactly. 'It seems odd that merely to watch the motion of
flight should give the body not only vicarious exhilaration

but release. So urgent is the rhythm that it invades the blood. This power of flight to take us in to itself through the eyes as though we had actually shared in the motion . . .' One of the heartening things about this approach to nature is that it is available to everyone. You do not need the books or the information to be taken into the life of a living being. You simply need to watch.

Reading Shepherd has helped me take the time to do that gazing, to allow my blood to be invaded and my body to 'share in the motion', but what I have also found is that the more I watch, the more I want to understand what I'm seeing. To enter the life of these creatures with deeper appreciation and insight, to *know* them, in more ways than one.

* * *

At the end of a long day wrestling with words and technology and feeling failed by both, I head out for a walk, planning to go a long way at a brisk pace to work off the frustrations. But no sooner am I in the woods on the other side of the railway line than a bird's call stops me. It's a new sound. Or, more probably, the first time I have noticed it, picking it out from the general chorus of twitters and cheeps on this July day. It's a high-pitched, two-note squeak, like the turning of a rusty wheelbarrow. I detect a flutter in the curtains of birch leaves and stand still, watching. The more I watch, the more I realise there are several birds darting through the canopy and across the thickets of the forest floor. And there's a second noise that strikes me now: an urgent, repeated *churrr* that sounds defensive. I can't figure out which calls belong to which flitting creatures, so I tug out my binoculars and scan the trees. Nothing moves. The wheelbarrow squeaks on, but I can only see a kaleidoscope of green. I lower the binos, and a bird shoots across the glade. I snap them back and search, but by the time I've adjusted the focus all I can see is the tremble of leaves where it has just disappeared. And hear the squeaking. I lower the binos again and hold my breath. Something small and dark nips into the edge of my vision, low down on a twig, but the slightest movement from me sends it off again. *Churr, churr.* Aha! So, the birds in the upper branches are the wheelbarrows and these lower ones are the rattlers. I feel a small surge of triumph. My detective nose is on the scent. But what are these birds? Can I identify them?

I tip-toe deeper into the glade as the first bird flies squeaking from tree to tree in a large circle around me and the little one dives off into the undergrowth. Sitting on the soft grass and moss, I pull out my notebook and scribble down what I've witnessed so far and watch and wait. The midsummer foliage is so thick that though the woods tremble with birdsong, it's incredibly difficult to get a good view of anything. The high one pauses long enough for me to catch it in the binos, but with the sun behind it, I only get a sense of size and shape. A slim creature, perhaps halfway between a chaffinch and a blackbird? It takes off again and when it lands on a branch opposite me, I get a fleeting glimpse of pale grey underparts and markings at the throat. It squeaks on and flies to the next tree, hidden. Meanwhile, the little bird has landed on the roots of a tree nearby and I manage to catch it in my sights, just a split-second before it scampers round the back. This is starting to feel like a game of cat and mouse. Honestly! I'm not trying to shoot you, I mutter, just look at you. Just learn your name.

As I watch these elusive birds, I am aware of two things. One is that their noise and behaviour can, no doubt, be explained by any number of things, from protecting young to seeking a mate. Yet at the same time, something in the way they keep vocalising, disappearing and re-appearing reminds me of the birds from some of my favourite children's books: the robin in *The Secret Garden* who holds the key to the hidden door, and the other robin in the snowy forest of Narnia who gets the children to follow him to the home of the beavers. In the stories, the children are drawn into a world they could not have imagined, a world of beauty and mystery where their lives are forever changed. Perhaps, in reality, my poor birds today are just trying to get rid of me, but I have a strong sense of being called. Here, in the woods so near my home, I am being coaxed out of my everyday not-seeing, not-knowing ignorance into a world of delight. Just like the worlds of *The Secret Garden* and Narnia, it is real and exists right alongside the world we occupy – is, indeed, a part of the same world – but its magic can be completely lost on us if we don't look, if we don't listen to the birds and follow them.

So, I stay there, watching and waiting, checking my bird book, gradually getting longer glimpses of my two summoners. And then I realise there are three. The low-down one is meeting another in brief, twittering snatches before they part again. I catch one of these encounters through the binoculars and realise it is feeding the other. A parent and chick! Aha, aha! With my sights prowling the undergrowth, I get a longer look at the chick. It is a ball of brown fluff with a pert tail sticking upright and an equally pert little bill. The initiated will know its identity at once – Nan Shepherd certainly did – but I am still a novice and forced to page through the likely suspects in the bird book. No . . . No . . . Maybe? No . . . YES! That's it! It's a wren! 'A WREN!' I almost holler to the woodland. 'I've found a wren! I've *recognised* a wren!' How can I describe the excitement of that discovery? Of that solving of the puzzle? Got you! I gloat, as I write the name in caps in my notebook. The wren hops on and *churr*s, oblivious. 'So tiny, so vital, with such volume of voice,' Shepherd wrote of wrens, who fly by 'in a whorl of joyful speed'. Now I know what she's talking about.

Meanwhile, in the branches above, the squeaking solo still circles around me as I twist and strain with the binoculars to catch the moments of rest. Who is the observer here and who observed? I realise I have become the centre of a forest arena, with the upper ring of the stalls inscribed by this bird, and the little wren family off in the wings. In what way do they see me, know me, name me? Invader? Threat? Monster? Gradually, I light on the upper bird often enough to note a tan colouring around the head and a striped effect at the throat. But it's too high and fast through the canopy for me to detect upper body colours and wing shape and my scouring of the bird book leaves me undecided. I note spotted flycatcher, whinchat, sedge warbler and tree pipit with question marks. I can hear the experienced twitchers choking on their tea. Probably Nan Shepherd, also. If only she were here to solve the puzzle in a trice. But then, maybe I wouldn't be working so hard to figure it out, wouldn't be watching and listening so well. Back home, studying online videos, I lean towards flycatcher. Sly little maybe-flycatcher. Not yet in the net of my naming, but definitely caught in my mind. Or am I the one who is hooked?

Shepherd knew her birds and *knew* them in ways deeper than the facts about them. 'They are not in the books for me,' she wrote. 'They are in living encounters, moments of their life that have crossed moments of mine.' But she writes about them with the full strength of both experience and information: two forces that continue to feed one another and yield ever deeper knowledge. I am still early in that marriage. The hunger to learn has many motives, from curiosity to shame. In Shepherd's novel *The Weatherhouse*, Ellen Falconer realises in her sixties that her life has been consumed by her fanciful imagination, leading her to false judgements and mistaken actions. Her epiphany comes when she cannot recognise a local bird and is filled with a sense of failure: '[A]s she sat miserably by her window she saw all at once that it was not only the bird's name of which she was ignorant: it was the whole world outside herself.' Determined to live a life of greater truth and awareness, she sets out to learn about the flora and fauna around her, 'to know their real selves that she might enter their life'. Her experiences resonate deeply with me. 'But her study halted. Birds moved so swiftly, she forgot so soon, her manuals were poor, and by her untaught efforts it was hard to identify these moving flakes of life and the bright, multitudinous flowers.' My own nature ID journey goes from stretches of daily observation and note-taking, which yield a growing and satisfying sense of grasp, to lapses of a week or more in which I feel everything I have learned has dissolved. Feathered friends become strangers again, with much the same sense of shame when I recognise someone in a supermarket but cannot remember their name or how I know them.

During a writing workshop in my residency with the national park, a lively discussion took off about the value of identification. One man was vehemently opposed to what he saw as a human-centred obsession with labelling. 'Why do we have to pin a name on everything? It's a kind of arrogance, going around reducing living creatures and growing things to Latin terms. This is a *blah-di-blah*, that's a *hoozi-wot*. Why can't you just experience it and appreciate it on its own terms?' It was a compelling argument and a new perspective for most of us; it certainly challenged me. What's in a name? Very little or almost everything. Names say as much about the person or group conferring the label as they do about the recipient, and most things have several names, reflecting the relationship between the namer and the named.

But what names do is give us a way of connecting our experiences with others. To discover more about wrens and share my observations, it is far easier using that name than my rambling, and perhaps misleading, descriptions. The name means nothing to the bird but everything to birdwatchers. It becomes a key to unlocking knowledge. But only partial knowledge. Simply memorising names, images and information about birds will never match the experience of close and patient observation. It will not 'invade the blood'. At the same time, the observation leads me back to the books. The name is no longer a label on packaging, but an identifier that summons a living being.

As Shepherd's character Ellen Falconer grew in her observations of the natural world, she grew also in her recognition of the importance of learning its particularities. 'Identify – discover their identity. She had never valued accurate information, holding that only the spirit signified, externals were an accident; yet when she found that by noting external details she could identify a passing bird or a growing plant, a thrill of joy passed through her heart. She was no longer captive within her single self.' Amen. Little by little, I too am being freed from the confines of my own head to look, listen and learn the distinctions of the natural world, and through that, to receive an inheritance of wonder.

Paradoxically, I am also learning not to be ashamed of my ignorance. I feel the eternal beginner, always seeking to get some kind of hold on the vast, teeming universe of life, but always trounced. It's an impossible task. I will never understand so much as the intricacies of a muddy puddle, far less the infinite, incomprehensible sweep of the stars and everything in between. But it doesn't matter. Of course I cannot master the world, because the very act of learning reveals the sheer extent of it. As Shepherd so beautifully expressed it, 'The thing to be known grows with the knowing.'

I am heartened by Robert Macfarlane's introduction to the 2011 edition of *The Living Mountain*, where he says, 'This is not a book that relishes its own discoveries; it prefers to relish its own ignorances.' Shepherd does not set out to educate the reader but to share with us her curiosity. The important thing, I have discovered with relief, is not to feel stupid, but open to learning; not defeated, but awed; not embarrassed, but humbled by delight. In his conversation with Krista Tippett on the On Being podcast, ornithologist and author Drew Lanham said, 'There's no shame in not knowing the name of a bird. At some point, as a scientist, it's important for me to be able to identify birds by accepted names, but then I revert frequently to what my grandmother taught me: the birds know who they are. They don't need you to tell them that . . . So seeing that bird, you can see all of these hues, and you can watch its behaviour, and you may hear it sing – well, in that moment, it's a beautiful thing, no matter what its name is. Just see the bird. Just see that bird.'

I look back on my years of Cairngorms wandering and realise that, despite my untuned ear and untrained eye, despite the poverty of my taxonomy, the world has poured out its gifts. And one of the main reasons I have been able to receive them has been the generosity of others. Though the best learning is done at the feet of nature herself – simply waiting, looking and listening – the journey is so much easier and richer with the help of those who are further along. Shepherd cites being guided by her naturalist friend 'who knew the hill better than I did then'. Like her, I have been blessed by the fellowship of experienced wildlife watchers, knowledgeable and patient experts – or even those who know just a little more than me – who have given of their time to help me see what was hidden in plain sight.

When Shepherd likens her discovery of the Cairngorms to pilgrimage, it invites multiple meanings. Though many pilgrims undertake a solitary journey, the traditional routes have been trod by thousands and are frequently walked in company. Even the solo traveller often stays at the communal rest houses along the way to share stories, advice, food and friendship. Though people set out for different reasons, seeking different gods or none at all, they rarely walk alone.

* * *

A year has passed since I began the writing of this book, and it is spring again. Very early spring, and because the Cairngorms are the highest area of Britain, and a good way north, we can be slow to unfurl from winter. Exactly a year ago, it was John, on my winter skills course on the mountain, who pointed out the snow buntings and a lone raven. This year, the temperatures have swung from minus twenty degrees in early February – with the lochs frozen so hard we could walk across them – to plus ten degrees within a week, and spring is hurtling in on a torrent of melt water and mild days. All of a sudden, the sky is alive with birdsong: the early chaffinch, the faithful robin, the tits in all their sizes and zestful colours, shooting from branch to branch, and piping with immoderate volume. The woodpecker's resonant drumming echoes around the woods, doves coo, crows gossip and an owl calls the night. I know it's a tawny owl because I asked my bird-listening friends. My heart lifts at the return of the dippy lapwings in the fields beside us, rising and plunging, swooping and sliding on invisible roller-coasters, unzipping the air with their wing-beat buzz. In Scots, they are called peewits, peesweeps and peasies, in a naming that evokes their sounds. Walking up on the ridge above Glenmore forest, we hear their cousins, the golden plover, whistling their piercing, two-note song. 'If there is one bird-call more than another that for me embodies the spirit of the mountain,' wrote Shepherd, 'it is the cry of the golden plover running in the bare and lonely places.'

But it's a fiendish, changeable season and we can return to sleet, snow and ice at any moment. The shepherds up here speak grimly of the 'lambing snows' in late March and early April. And each time it thaws again, the earth looks forlorn. 'I think the plateau is never quite so desolate as in some days of early spring,' Shepherd wrote, 'when the snow is rather dirty, perished in places like a worn dress.' I walk out on a grey March day when that departed snow has left the grass crushed and dank, the sky menacing and the loch heavy as lead. From the southern end, the voices of whooper swans rise in a bike-horn clanging as they beat towards me and land in a spray of water. Sun breaks through the cloud and sets a bare tree on fire; out on the loch, the swans drift into the unearthly light.

It was our friend Mark, violinist and wildlife guide, who first taught us how to distinguish the whooper swan from the mute, and who knew the songs of birds so well he wrote them down in musical notation. He was also our usher into the world of the ospreys, telling us their story as we peered through his telescope. Once persecuted to extinction in the British Isles, these migratory birds of prey began their come-back in the 1950s, which is presumably why they do not feature in *The Living Mountain*. Arriving from West Africa around the first week of April, they return to the same nests above the Cairngorms lochs, adding more structure each time and fighting to defend mate, home and young. As my eyes have been opened, I have witnessed the male spear down to snatch fish, deliver them to the female in the nest, and perform his sky dance above her. Still endangered and fiercely beautiful, with their fire-gold eyes and hooked beaks, they are the royalty of the loch, here in their summer palace, our jewels in the crown. The spring after Mark shared their mysteries with us, he was diagnosed with a brain tumour, and two years later, he died. As he was lowered into the earth of the churchyard below the nest, the newly returned ospreys soared above.

By summer, we are teeming with birds, the air rippling with their voices. Shape-shifting beings of colour and sound, they move between water, sky, earth and tree like circus performers – the ducks, geese and swans, the waders, warblers and wanderers, the birds of prey and passage – quivering, diving, soaring, plummeting, declaring their presence through songs, wing beats, shaking leaves and splashing water. Martins, swifts, swallows, curlews, oystercatchers, finches, sandpipers, lapwings and countless more. But as Shepherd says, 'Why should I make a list?' The names have a poetic beauty, but their meaning lies in the real, living things and the moments they have crossed our paths.

Most of the Cairngorms birds congregate in the waterways, forests and fields of the strath. One August, my friend Suzi took me to a lochan wreathed with lily pads where she pointed out a softly pacing moorhen and a family of Slavonian grebes, both parents to-ing and fro-ing in the rushes with silver fish in their beaks for the ravenous chicks. The small, brown dipper, on the other hand, can be at home in the rivers and burns all the way from the valley floor right up into the hills. He looks an unassuming bird, even timid, as he bobs on the spot on a rock. But suddenly he is a magician, walking right under the water for his food, caped in 'a film of light'.

Meanwhile, higher up on the rocky slopes and plateau, the elusive ptarmigan walk stealthily over rocks, camouflaged in their mottled summer feathers. Summer also brings the lovely dotterel, whose apparent mildness belies their grit, as they migrate thousands of miles to raise their brood on the wind-savaged tops. It is usually the male that incubates the eggs, and one day on Carn Ban Mor, when the plateau seemed devoid of life, I saw one tucked in a hollow in the grass, still as a stone till a breeze ruffled his feathers.

And, always, there are the meadow pipits, those small, air-bouncing balls of song that trapeze around you on a summer walk; and the swifts, the creatures that Shepherd says 'make visible and audible some essence of the free, wild spirit of the mountain'.

* * *

Year round, we have the deer, which were such a source of fascination to Shepherd. The gentle roe are often in the forests near my home, slipping without sound through the shafts of sunlight between the trees, their ashy fur and slender legs the same colour and shape as the birch. Sometimes, I slowly become aware that a roe is there, staring at me, and both of us stand motionless, till her ear flickers, and she is away. The red deer, meanwhile, gather in the folds of moor and mountain, the hinds elegant and watchful, the stags rearing their rough heads, crowned with antlers. When they run, I am always startled by their speed and power, their ease in leaping drystone dykes and ploughing across rocky rapids. 'They seem to float,' Shepherd says, 'yet their motion is in a way more wonderful even than flight, for each of these gleaming hooves does touch the ground.' The sight of a herd flowing up a slope is mesmerising, though the sound of their roar in the autumn rut would put the fear of God in you.

Among our smaller resident mammals, one of the most enchanting is the red squirrel, threatened by the advance of the non-native grey, but gradually regaining ground.

Though I have never touched one, I wish I could, as their fur looks smooth as satin while their tail is an explosion of fluffy softness. But be not deceived, these small creatures can outwit the most cunning birdfeeder defences, and are swift and strong in their race across open ground and up trees, their coppery bodies fluid as water and bright as flame. Shepherd describes getting ever closer to a young squirrel, busy foraging, till it startles and runs up a tree 'and jeers down at me in triumph'.

Equally lithe are the pine martens, though much harder to spot. I have only seen one, thanks to a local guide and a secret hide at night where the marten slipped out from the dark trees to take the food offering, its long body almost serpentine, its face delicate and keen.

And there are the countless tiny creatures, the insects and beetles, moths and butterflies, worms and wonders too small to see. Halfway up a hill, once, I'm waylaid by an anthill at the side of the path. Made of red Scots pine needles and the size of an upturned bucket, it is a seething mass of activity, all the minute, moving backs glittering like beads. And by late summer, the mounds of heather are decked with spider webs, a silver-grey lace spangled with dew.

Through the autumn, many of the birds leave us again. The ospreys vanish in September, one at a time, with the chicks going last and, by some mystery we may never fathom, finding their path all the way to West Africa. The skies ring with skeins of geese, mainly the greylag and the pink-footed, their formations rippling across the blue like pennants in the wind. Shepherd wrote how on '[o]ne blustering October day I watched an arrow-head of them, twenty-seven birds in perfect symmetry, flying south down the valley in which I stood'.

Finally, we are left with our faithful ones. The unsung buzzard, familiarity breeding contempt, but no less beautiful to me, especially in his soulful cry. The rooks that rise in gusts from the great oaks by the loch, a fury of wings and squabbling, only to settle again into the same branches, carrying on their ceaseless wittering. The common mallards, upending in the rushes, the iridescent green of their heads a daily wonder. The grey heron, that flies up the River Spey with an abrasive croak, a long bird, all pointy beak, elbows and knees, like a living missile firing north. Flocks of gulls careering overhead in a chorus of rusty, sea-side calls, as murmurations of starlings unfold the skies. On a quiet, grey morning, a local birdwatcher of vast knowledge, Dave, kindly meets me on a nearby shore and draws back the curtains of the loch, pointing out birds and behaviours that were otherwise invisible to me. The flurry of wood pigeons in flight; the spritely tufted ducks diving and shaking their heads; the wondrous goldeneye with whistling wings. The secret scripture is read aloud, its hidden text made known.

Then winter comes, hushed by snow and cold. So much wildlife has fled or hunkered down that it can be harder to see things, but all the more rewarding. A day at the end of December, on a snowbound ridge in the Cairngorms, with cloud swirling and dissolving, we see ptarmigan again, but this time in their winter whites. They come catapulting out from behind rocks, their swift flight and croak the only sound on the mountain, their wings beating so fast they form a translucent, feathered globe, 'like an aura of light around the body'. In the hidden gullies of the winter hills, mountain hares break cover and pelt up the slope, white as the snow but for the dark ears, the button eyes and nose and a smoky tinge across the back.

Far up Glen Feshie in late winter, another wildlife guide and friend, Duncan, trains his telescope on a patch of snowy ground beside pine forest. There, I see black grouse for the first time, and even better, they are performing their lek, the male combat dance of dominance to win the females watching from the trees. Further up the glen, he points out two ravens on a high branch and explains their mutual preening. For all the world, it looks like a kiss.

And further still, we sit in sunshine over lunch and conversation, waiting for my first, longed-for sighting of what Shepherd calls 'the king of birds'. On my own, I would not have known where to look for any of these birds and not recognised what I was seeing. A good wildlife guide is a kind of seer, a sage who knows the passage of living creatures, can predict their coming and take you to the place of revelation. But he is no wizard and cannot summon them at will. They are, after all, wild. All the greater the exhilaration, then, when, high above the snowy crags, a great bird appears. Its wings beat, beat and glide; beat, beat and glide. Another soars in to meet it. And then a third. Even from a distance, I can see 'the power in the flight that enthrals the eye' and how they catch the sun on their feathers. And I can hear my guide name them. Golden eagles.

At last, I have seen them. And I am not alone.

IX.

AIR & LIGHT

As I watch, the light comes pouring round the edges of the shapes that stand against the sky, sharpening them till the more slender have a sort of glowing insubstantiality, as though they were themselves nothing but light.

What Shepherd brought to the Cairngorms was revelation. She did not so much describe a glorious mountain range, as focus the lens of her perception on a seemingly ordinary mountain range and unveil its glory. Many of her experiences were not spectacular or impressive, at least not at first glance, because that is the essential nature of the Cairngorms. Their treasures are often secret, their lights dimmed. But it was in her slow and patient gaze that the hidden fires were revealed. This is expressed with particular power in her chapter 'Air and Light'. 'But even in this scene of grey desolation,' she writes of an ugly day, 'if the sun comes out and the wind rises, the eye may suddenly perceive a miracle of beauty. For on the ground the down of a ptarmigan's breast feather has caught the sun.' To see and express how such 'magical and lovely light' fills the earth was a driving force in her life and writing.

As I read *The Living Mountain* and learn to read the

text of this enigmatic range with her help, it is not just the Cairngorms that have changed, but something in me. In my opening chapter, I complained about the cold, wind and wet of Scotland, even more so when they come at me like a trio of savage trolls with their fists balled. But it's not as simple as that. In a strange, counter-intuitive way, I do love rain. Especially when it pours down in droplets so big and hard it sounds like hail and bounces off the ground. Especially when it sweeps in from an electric sky on billows of thunder, the heavens cracked with lightning, the air smelling of wild winds. Especially when it reminds me of monsoon in mountains. And, yes, I love wind, too. It can be thrilling when it scoops me up like a kid in laughter, when it roars in trees and crashes in waves and upends the sky. Wind – when it does not wreak destruction or bring death – shakes me to life. And even the cold. The cold, too, can be borne when it comes with the glitter of snow and ice crystals and air so clear it snaps. When it freezes the loch to marble and sends the skaters out in sweeping glides. Yes, I realise to my own surprise, I can even love the cold. So, if it is not the rain of Scotland that really gets me, or the wind, or the cold, what is it?

It's the dark. It's the day after day of low, grumbling grey cloud; that dithering about whether to rain or not to rain; that lowering, looming, glooming that saps the world and my spirit of colour.

When my boys were tiny and we lived in Stirling, two of my good friends were a fellow Aussie and a Kiwi, both married to Scots. We regularly exchanged notes. 'I hate the feeling,' one said, 'that the sky is always sitting right on my head.' And we all agreed, noisily. That winter I gradually sank into a darkness of every shade of bleak. I was homesick for sunny, colourful Nepal, which we had left in the July, just weeks before the arrival of our second son; I was missing my family, who were all in Kathmandu; I was struggling with a lively two-year-old and wakeful baby, overwhelmed by the intensity of love and needs, both theirs and mine. By mid-December, it felt like someone had turned out the lights, my exhausted days going from black at eight a.m. to heavy grey as I pushed the pram down grubby pavements in search of company, till all went black again at four in the afternoon. When I confessed to my GP that I was depressed, tears spilling onto my baby's head, she simply said, 'I am not surprised.'

Alistair and I wrote a list of everything that might help, and one of them was a light box. It was painfully expensive and bulky for a small flat, but there it stood on the kitchen table, or the desk beside our bed, and beamed its 10,000 lux rays at me for any minutes I could steal in front of it. And it did help. Gradually, I surfaced from that winter of darkness, and the light came back.

I don't imagine the Scottish sky has changed much in the twenty years since then, but I know my head has. I only occasionally use the light box now, and only for excessive tiredness in the depths of winter, rather than depression. And though I still find cloudy days dull, especially several together, they no longer dominate my experience of the weather in the way they once did. I have acclimatised; I have come to appreciate the movement in a seemingly flat cloud and the textures and gradations of grey. Shepherd wrote in her essay titled 'The Colours of Deeside' in *The Deeside Field*, 'Our grey land, our grey skies, hold poised within them a thousand shades of colour.' I have, at last, learned to see them, to watch the sky and find there a theatre of change.

This is partly because the upper strath of the Spey, where we now live, has a lower average rainfall than most of Scotland. We get a clearer vision, and I am eternally grateful. Our kitchen window has views across trees to the sunsets in the west and when I lean out the dormer in our upstairs bedroom, I can see over rooftops to the Monadhliaths on my left, fields and forest ahead and the Cairngorms to the east. And above them all, the great, singing sky. I still adore the summer when the light carries on and on and we start to wander outside barefoot, doors and windows hanging open, grass and bugs drifting in as books and mugs drift out. But I have also come to love the transformations of air and light year round, from the lengthening shadows and deepening colours of autumn, through the metallic glints of winter, to the hopeful dawning of spring. Now I don't know which season I love best, but I do know the sky of Scotland no longer sits on my head; it fills it.

Being in the Cairngorms in high summer is a communion with sky. Long before we know the forecast, we ring-fence four days in August for walking into the mountains from Deeside, my first time following the route of Shepherd's first major ascent. Wonderfully, when the time comes, the weather is clear and warm and we happily pack sunscreen and shorts. As we take the sandy trail up Glen Lui, the early cloud clears to sunshine and lights the curving hills, blushed to mauve by the wide sweeps of heather in full bloom. We don't know if it's a consequence of less air pollution because of lockdowns, but everyone testifies to the abundance and depth of colour in the wild plants of 2020. Fat bees root into the round purple heads of scabious, as buttercups, hawksweed and bird's-foot trefoil bring flashes of bright yellow. We can hear the clear whistle of willow warblers and see a stonechat on a fence post, smart as a footman in his uniform of black, white and russet. Like Shepherd, we walk through the thick mounds of heather at the side of the trail, stirring clouds of pollen and its sweet honey fragrance into the soft air. 'For as the feet brush the bloom . . . one walks surrounded by one's own aura of heather scent.' If it wasn't for her, I would have just trudged on the gravel and missed this pleasure.

An hour along the track, the once-elegant Derry Lodge is now boarded up and home only to a colony of house martins, swooping in and out of its eaves and through the tall trees around. Here we turn north up Glen Derry, where the path rises gently through regenerating Scots pine forest, carpeted in wildflowers, grasses and mosses. This is part of the Mar Lodge Estate, owned by the National Trust for Scotland and undergoing a similar transformation to Glen Feshie.

Butterflies settle on the blooms as blue dragonflies catch the sun in their zippy flight over bog pools. By late morning, we're thirsty and sweaty, and when we spot a swimming hole through the trees, the chattering pull of the Derry Burn becomes irresistible. We scramble down for fifty metres through the scrub and gladly dump our heavy packs where the burn spills over boulders into a sheltered pool. 'I like the unpath best,' said the young daughter of Shepherd's friend, and it's clear she did too. Channelling ever more of her spirit, I strip naked and wade in. The water is cold on hot skin but brings delight in the rush of sensation, the pounding of the waterfall and pull of the current, the patterns of light and colour on the surface and the stones beneath. We eat lunch on the sunbaked rocks at the edge, glad we planned an itinerary with enough time for the unplanned. 'Haste can do nothing with these hills,' Shepherd said. Haste can do nothing with life, I believe, though must learn the lesson over and over again.

After the dip, the climb beyond the tree-line gets steeper, the day hotter, the packs heavier. In South Asia and Australia, I was used to the cloudless midday sky feeling relentless and uncompromising, but I had not expected it in Scotland. 'I have heard of a strange delusion that the sun does not shine up here,' wrote Shepherd. 'It does; and because of the clarity of the air its light has power.' We stop outside the Hutchison Memorial Hut intending to brew tea, but the whole place is swarming with midges and we toil on.

A party of five come stomping raucously down the trail, all brown and shirtless except for the one woman, in a black singlet. First up is a weathered, white-haired man in lime green nylon work trousers who offers us wine gums and, forgetting the Covid pandemic, we both dip into the sweaty packet and take one. They are path builders, who dig and heave stones into place year round, whether shovelling snow out of the way or sweating through a day like this, their work often involving hours of walking at the top and tail of each day. This is Friday and they invite us to their party in Glen Shee that night, but we're heading in the opposite direction. Watching them pound off down the slope in waves of jokes and laughter, I marvel that after a week of walking and working in hot sun, they have energy for a party. Clearly made of tougher stuff than me.

Resting on a rock well above the midges, we snack on nuts and watch the long strips of cloud shadow sliding across the corrie walls. Beside the path, there are pools in the peat bog where tiny water boatmen skate across the surface. Grasses and wildflowers rise at the fringes, the delicate yellow bog asphodel like totems, the mounds of moss in colours like the path builder's sweets. At one angle, the bog water is black, at another, gleaming silver and slick as glass, while at another, it's a fallen piece of bright blue sky. 'The eye sees what it didn't see before, or sees in a new way what it had already seen.'

It's four in the afternoon when we crest the lip into Corrie Etchachan and stand gazing on the scene that so astounded Shepherd, because it is not a mountain's summit but an interior. 'And what an interior! the boulder-strewn plain, the silent shining loch, the black overhang of its precipice, the drop to Loch Avon and the soaring barricade of Cairn Gorm beyond, and on every side, except where we had entered, towering mountain walls.'

Although she also came in summer, hers was a foggy day and her guide led her straight on up to Ben Macdui, the trail quickly disappearing into snow and the loch into white cloud. Our day is unusually warm and still for the Cairngorms, and after our slog with heavy packs, it doesn't take long to strip and wade in. There are other campers and walkers on the horizon, though, so I don a swimsuit. The water is even colder than the Derry pool, but not freezing, and we swim for several minutes, bodies thrumming with the joy of being in this high bowl of water, suspended in rock, in sky, in light. There are flashes of bright blue on the gravel bottom, and I dive down to get one of the sapphire stones, but when lifted out of the water, it proves to be simply white quartzite with black speckles. There is not a hint of blue. Something in the play of water and light gives it that unearthly shade, so I carry it home and keep it on my desk as a reminder of magic.

We set up the tent above the loch where the ground is drier and we can catch a light breeze from the north. Camping in the Cairngorms usually requires finding shelter from wind, but on still, warm days, the priority is escaping midges. Drinking tea in the late sun, we watch gossamer tendrils of mist coiling up from the Loch Avon chasm, dissolving over Loch Etchachan and reforming against the dark crags on the opposite side. I bring rice to the boil and wrap the pot in a sleeping bag to continue cooking while I heat the curry. I neglect to communicate this cunning plan to Alistair, however, who accidentally knocks it over, spilling rice and starchy water through the tent. Mercifully, the down bags and our marriage are spared. Our 'curry' is a mash-up of leftover daal, two curries, a tin of beans and two barbequed sausages; it's amazing what you will eat in the high hills after a day of walking and swimming. Squatting in front of the stove, I feel midges needling around my face and up the back of my shirt, and by the time we've eaten, they are a decided nuisance. To avoid them and settle our dinner, we stride across the boulder field to the north, passing under the shadow of the crag, the sunlight slipping away ahead of us. We stand at the opening above Loch Avon, on the opposite side from where we had climbed down to swim the previous year. The stretch of dark water lies hundreds of feet below us now, deep in its ravine of silence and shadow, while the cliff tops around are fired by the late sun.

On the way back, we inspect the plants of the boulder field: the deep green shoots of the heather – without flower at this altitude – the delicate pink blooms of the mountain azalea, the yellow bog asphodel, the tufts of blaeberry leaves, the mosses and lichens. These include the other-worldly 'fairy cups' of the *Cladonia fimbriata,* tiny scoops the size of thumb tacks, on top of thin stems, sometimes with red balls nestled in them. The sprays of deep red deer grass with golden tips look like fireworks, and the nodding heads of the longer grasses are weavings of light. I am struck by the juniper that, lower down, can be the size of a man, but up here grows flat and creeping like ground cover; its scent is so sharp and tangy – what Shepherd called 'a delectable fragrance' – that I snap off a piece in the hope that burning it might ward off the midges.

No such luck. The wind has completely dropped, and the midges are now so bad that we can't stay still long enough to thicken our custard on the stove; we are reduced to pouring it, pale and watery, over slabs of ginger cake and eating our dessert while pacing around like caged beasts. We wash up and clean teeth as quickly as possible, wishing we had the multiple arms of a Hindu deity for simultaneously doing tasks and swatting. Despite lashings of repellent all evening and a furious attempt at brushing them off, by the time I dive into the tent, I am a seething continent of midges. They colonise the folds of the tent and my clothing, crawling into my hair and riding in on my breath till I am coughing them back up. Lying in the soupy half-light, sticky from Smidge, sunscreen and sweat, constantly crushing the little fiends, I listen to a soft pattering on the fly cover. It sounds like the lightest drops of rain, but is no less than the landing of midges, an invasion of tiny aliens gathering forces just inches away. Sleep is poor and fitful: I'm cramped and sliding down the slope, longing to be outside in the endless light, but held siege by this incongruous, vengeful army. Though stiff, hot and desperate to pee, I don't dare open the flap.

By morning, my body is peppered with bites and there is now a crawling plague massed and waiting on the tent mesh. We prepare a co-ordinated exit, count down, and eject ourselves into the swarm. With much cursing and swiping, we shove stove and breakfast things into a sack and hightail it up the ridge of Beinn Mheadhoin. As soon as we are moving fast on higher ground, the beasts fall away and it strikes me, not for the first time, that in all her writing on the Cairngorms, Nan Shepherd never mentions this. *The Living Mountain* references midges only once, in an extended passage where she lists dozens of creatures in an exaltation of delight, ending with the phrase 'life in so many guises'. Although throughout the book she insists that the ugliness and horrors of the mountain are equally essential to its nature, at no point do these include being eaten alive by these minute savages.

Our mountain guide friend, John, offers an explanation: back then, you never got midges high up in the Cairngorms, in fact, not even forty years ago, when he was first exploring the range. This is hotly disputed, I discover, when I put the question to Twitter a few days later, with some hoary old-timers insisting the midges have always been up there and always in those numbers. I'm inclined to trust John, whose embodied knowledge of the Cairngorms runs far and deep.

The same change is true of ticks, the nasty little blood-sucking insects that carry Lyme disease. Local shepherds and moorland managers, who expend considerable cost and energy suppressing ticks, say that you rarely found them above 1,000 feet a generation ago.

It is suggested that the rising of both scourges is down to climate change, as Scotland gets both warmer and wetter; as such, I am reluctant to embrace them as part of the essential nature of the mountain and more likely to curse them as yet another sign of human error. Shepherd recognised the connectedness of all things on the mountain – indeed, in life – and how we are part of an intricate and inter-dependent web of relationships. 'The mountain is one and indivisible,' she insisted. This is evident not only when natural processes are in harmony and good working order, but also when they are damaged.

As we head up the ridge, the sun steals into the absolute quiet and stillness of Corrie Etchachan, up the far side from where it slipped away last night. It sparkles on the lightly scored surface of the loch and inhabits the dewdrops on the wet grasses, turning them to a mesh of gold. We pass the buckets and spades of the path builders up to the first tor on the top, where we stop for breakfast. Up here, the light is so sharp that every rock face and tiny leaf looks laser cut. This quality of air is something that struck me about Scotland from the beginning, how the same skies could one day be thick and heavy with cloud, yet on another, wide open and clear, the sun knifing through like diamond. I concur with Shepherd: 'Light in Scotland has a quality I have not met elsewhere.' And it is that light, piercing even the shortest days of December, that has won my peace with the Scottish weather. From here, the tops of the great range rise in sculpted lines, their northern flanks still holding rare patches of snow, pearly in the morning sun. Far below us, Loch Avon is a sliver of black. We wander across the ridge in the wake of meadow pipits swooping and singing. Far away, in every direction, the valleys are lost in a sea of cloud.

Back at the campsite, the rearguard of the midges is still mounting a final campaign, but there is enough bright sun and breeze to help fend them off as we throw together a packed lunch and break camp, shaking a black confetti out of our tent. Two other tents shared the shores of Loch Etchachan last night and there are now several walkers across the corrie and even a party of mountain bikers skittering down the scree. Before leaving, we have another swim, this time longer and deeper. Mosses gather on the loch floor in thick rugs of greens and blacks, and when I run my hands through them, plumes of bubbles rise around me. Pushing out of my depth, something large and pale looms up ahead, a fleshy monster in the wavering water-light. I know nothing of that size could exist way up here, but it's unnerving. Getting closer, I realise it's a massive granite boulder, just submerged and glowing soft pink. I climb onto it and, rising up into the sharp air, it feels like I am walking on water and standing on time.

Later, we make the long, steep plod up the pyramid of Derry Cairngorm. From a distance, all the rocks of its scree slope appear the same dull grey, but up close, like the skies, they refract into a kaleidoscope of colours, textures and patterns: the dusky pinks, salmons and reds of the exposed granite, the blues and greys of its weathered face and the faceted white quartz and flecks of sparkling mica. Over these, the flat splatterings of lichens, in their charcoals and greens, are clear and surprising as paint. Author and artist John Ruskin said, '[A] stone, when it is examined, will be found to be a mountain in miniature.' The haul to the top is rewarded by far-flung views. Cloud still fills the distant plains, and the mountains that rise from it look like faraway islands, higher and haughtier than when tied to land. 'Far off, another peak lifts like a small island from the smother,' wrote Shepherd, of a similar scene. We recognise the sweeping curve of Lochnagar and the double-hump of Beinn a' Ghlò.

Back on the ridge above Loch Etchachan, our route picks up the Ben Macdui trail, passing springs thick with bright mosses and liverworts in shades of lime, scarlet and plum, all their quiet water seeping down to a burn in the fold of the hill. Stopping at a rocky spur looking south across the plunging drop of Coire Sputan Dearg, we stare out at the vast sweep of stone and sky. The clouds are now enormous – downy heaps of white – and behind them, the sky spans every shade from pale sea-glass green on the northern horizon to turquoise, to bright aqua, to cobalt and finally an intense ultramarine directly overhead. Under this endless canopy of blue, the mountains flow out around us, their curves, hollows and crests swelling and falling like breakers in a giant sea, lit by the sun. Filling all the spaces between the air.

'The air is part of the mountain,' Shepherd wrote, 'which does not come to an end with its rock and soil.' Invisible in itself, it is easy to think of it as emptiness, or not to think of it at all, but I have learned from a paragliding friend just how much substance and movement it holds. Gliders learn to read the air like skiers read snow and canoeists read rivers. They look for dark surfaces on the ground that will warm the air and make it rise; they see leaves trembling and sense the subtle shifts in thermal currents; they watch the birds. Ah, birds, those athletes of air. Birds, like the golden eagle, who can ride it in slow, rising spirals or in seemingly endless sailing with just the barest movement of wings. In awe of the eagle, Shepherd saw its 'power which binds the strength of the wind to its own purpose'. Birds carry a map of the sky so intuitive and fluid that it can only be read because every instinct and fibre of their being is in perfect tune. Theirs is the miracle of flight.

On this day with no wind, the air is suddenly parted by meadow pipits flying low across the ground, chirping through their tumbling, plummeting, soaring dance. Observing how these glorious displays of flight must arise in direct response to the demands of the mountain, Shepherd concluded that 'beauty is not adventitious but essential'. Such plain-looking little creatures in their soft brown and ivory, pipits never cease to astonish me with their exaltation in movement and song. As swiftly as they appeared, they vanish again, the curtains of air folding back to quiet. It turns my head from the far view of giant things to the close gaze at the diminutive and fragile. Here, a butterfly hovers among the rocks, a small dark tremble in the expanse of stillness. Somewhere, a ptarmigan croaks. Its voice falls away into a deep well of silence. It is a long time before I can move.

Our camp is on a grassy shelf near the edge of the ridge, higher and more exposed than last night, where we hope to harness the lower temperatures and likely breezes in our defence against the midges. A rare patch of level ground, big enough for a handful of tents, and with stones gathered into low shelter walls, it is clearly a well-used spot. Perhaps it's the one Shepherd chose when she took family friends, the Sutherland children, up the mountain in 1946. According to their younger brother, Malcolm, they had returned 'full of their adventure – how they had slept out, during the short summer night, on the plateau behind Ben MacDhui'. They did not, I note, mention midges.

Just below the site, the burn we have followed up the ridge spreads across gravel into a shallow pool, fringed by the prints of deer. I lie down to wash off the sweat, insect repellent and sunscreen, finding water at the edges that is almost warm from the day's sun, whereas the central channel is deeply cold. This is because it flows down from a remaining snow bed about a hundred metres above, and after dinner we walk up to investigate.

Most years, there are patches of snow in the Cairngorms that outlast the summer, and Shepherd wrote of touching them with awe, believing them to be eternal. But in the warm summer of 1933, they disappeared altogether. 'Antiquity has gone from our snow,' she lamented. And, no doubt, lamented again when they vanished in 1959. She did not live to see their more frequent dissolution in recent years, but among those who take note are Iain Cameron, who makes a detailed annual study of Scotland's snow beds and has recorded their sobering decline. After the disappearance in 2022 of The Sphinx, the Cairngorms snow patch which is usually Scotland's most tenacious, he said, 'The Sphinx has now vanished four times in the last six years, having done so only five times in the last 300 . . . The future for semi-permanent snows in Scotland looks bleak.'

We scoop some of the snow into our hands. Partially melted and refrozen, its crystals are knobby and clear, like ice. Nearby, a clump of moss campion is in full bloom, its exquisite pink flowers so fragile yet feisty, here at the brink of snow, wind and uncompromising rock. Shepherd called it 'the most startling of all the plateau flowers', marvelling at its strong roots and resilience, how some large patches 'must have endured the commotion of many winters'.

Back at our camp we sit for the longest time watching the light change on the north-eastern ridges, the shadows sharpening and deepening, cloaking the hills in smoky blue as breaths of cloud rise and retreat. The tors on Beinn Mheadhoin look one moment as strong as hill forts, and at the next, wreathed in mist like the castles of a magical kingdom, till finally caving in to shadow and ruin. Shepherd's

'Poem IX' is entirely about the sunset on that ridge:

> What strange complicity of earth
> With what bright god is here.

As the last of the sun runs like a lick of flame up the mountain, there is an enormous quiet, a silence that is not empty but brim full, a holy hush in which even the birds are still and the only sound is the faint trickle of the burn. It is like the evening of creation. 'Up on the plateau, light lingers incredibly far into the night, long after it has left the rest of the earth. Watching it, the mind grows incandescent and its glow burns down into deep and tranquil sleep.'

We wake to the early light and unzip the tent, looking directly north-east. The sky is a luminous wash of pastels, touched by a sliver of moon. Its shining span hangs above the sharp outline of hills and an ocean of low, white cloud. As we wait for the sun, the tent flaps caught back in their toggles become the drapes of a theatre stage for a play whose acts we know but whose performance is different every time. By 5.30, a hidden fire begins kindling on the far rim of the clouds and the dark grasses beside us turn copper. Liquid orange breaks upwards like magma rising through smoke, and it echoes the magma that made the Cairngorms. Like Shepherd, '[T]here I lie on the plateau, under me the central core of fire from which was thrust this grumbling, grinding mass of plutonic rock, over me blue air, and between the fire of the rock and the fire of the sun, scree, soil and water, moss, grass, flower and tree, insect, bird and beast, wind, rain and snow – the total mountain.'

X.

LIFE: MAN

Yet so long as they live a life close to their wild
land, subject to its weathers, something of its
own nature will permeate theirs. They will be
marked men.

When Nan Shepherd devoted an entire chapter of *The Living Mountain* to 'Man', it reflected her belief that the human is as much a part of the place as every other element. 'All are aspects of one entity, the living mountain.' She explored how people and mountain have shaped one another, for better or worse, down through time. In particular, she wrote with profound admiration of the crofters, estate workers and other hill folk who opened their homes and guided her in the Cairngorms. 'These people are bone of the mountain,' she said, but also acknowledged that their precarious way of life, with its subsistence farming and primitive living conditions, was 'hard and astringent'. While staying with them and joining in the basic chores of life – drawing water from a well and breaking sticks for the cooking fire – she experienced a 'deep pervasive satisfaction' but steered shy of romanticising. That 'slowing down the tempo of life' might be pleasurable in the short term for the city visitor, but drudgerous as an unceasing demand. She understood why many of the young folk wanted to leave, though not all. 'Some of them love these wild places with devotion and ask nothing better than to spend their lives in them.' Either way, even within her lifetime, that existence was disappearing.

Today, not many people still live in the higher locations that she described, and farming practices are radically changed. Some of the humble cottages and bothies she stayed in have been renovated into expensive holiday houses, while others are crumbling. Some still accommodate estate staff, though in mercifully more modern and comfortable style. Descendants from the characters she mentions are still around, but no longer in those homes. It may have saddened her, but she was realistic about change and respectful of people's needs to find a sustainable life.

Her chapter, however, is about far more than just the people who lived and worked in the lower slopes of the Cairngorms. It begins with her sitting all alone on a silent plateau after a day of meeting no one. 'Man might be a thousand years away. Yet, as I look around me, I am touched at many points by his presence.' She goes on to number the many signs of human interaction with the range, from paths to shelters to the map in her hands. However much she loved to retreat to the mountains for solitude and restoration, she held no illusions about them as untouched wilderness. But within their sprawling mass, she nevertheless became a master at finding places 'off the recognised route to any particular destination', the roads less travelled, the 'unpaths'.

One of the best of these is Coire Garbhlach. Its name means 'a rough place' and from above and below, it looks impenetrable. A steep, twisting valley, it cuts into the western side of the Feshie hills, its overlapping folds offering no portal and no glimpse of its treasures. It has been quietly drawing me for some time, for no other reason than its secretive allure. You don't hear much about it, unlike the more famous Cairngorms destinations, but the snippets I had heard were intriguing: an abandoned track, unusual wildflowers, a waterfall.

On the June day we set out to penetrate its mystery, we are welcomed by three brown hares pounding off into the bushes ahead of us, their long bodies and legs gangly pistons of power. The infinite sky is vivid with sunlight, huge, humpy cumulus clouds surfing the blue like giant schooners, their sails pluming. Most of the walk into the corrie demands pushing through shin-deep heather or picking a way up the rocks around Allt Garbhlach burn, and this is only possible because a long dry spell has limited the flow to a pleasant tumble. At other times, snow melt and heavy rain can render it a violent torrent and the valley completely inaccessible. We pass plantation forest and a scattering of ancient Scots pines. Any sign of a path disappears, and it is clear how few people come this way. It was once a stalking route, but a wide Land Rover track up the neighbouring valley has assumed that role.

At the opening of the corrie, the stream bed is a good twenty metres wide, the water splitting and joining in its meandering through the stones. Sunshine floods it, making the rocks at the bottom radiate all the warm shades of coral, amber and gold, some speckled and glinting, a few in contrasting greys and blacks. Shepherd's poem 'The Hill Burns' describes Cairngorms streams as 'Fiercely pure / Transparent as light.' The trees soon fall away and most of the hillside is matted with old dry heather, broken by patches of scree. Sometimes we find narrow deer tracks through the foliage, our arrival sending meadow pipits darting into the air, but the trails keep disappearing and it's easier to follow the stream bed. In the warmth and the steady climb, it is a delight to hear the cool rush of the burn and to kneel down and drink whenever we need. 'The sound of all this moving water is as integral to the mountain as pollen to the flower,' Shepherd wrote.

And flowers themselves are equally integral. The further up we go, the more we see. This valley is unusual in the Cairngorms as most of its rocks are the older schists that pre-date the granite. The different soils this generates, and the wind shelter afforded by its steep, zig-zagging shape, mean Coire Garbhlach harbours a distinctive range of wildflowers. I am stopped in my tracks over and over again by another vision of loveliness at my boots: thistles, campions, bog asphodel, St John's wort, Arctic azalea, mossy saxifrage, water avens, foxgloves, wild mountain thyme and roseroot. Tiny and fragile blooms, with intricate details and vivid colours, so bright and brave in this cleft of wilderness. As Shepherd says of the flowers, their 'way of life lies in the mountain's way of life as water lies in a channel'. Among them, we see a slick, dappled frog sunning itself on a bare rock and fritillary butterflies chasing each other in a blur of wings. Damselflies flash in vivid blues as tiny insects dart above the water like skittering points of light. In this place of hulking mountains and big weather, there is untold delight in the smallest things. There is also the reminder that the fate of even the least of these will affect the greatest.

* * *

In Shepherd's foreword to *The Living Mountain*, two of the changes she notes in the previous thirty years are that '[t]he Nature Conservancy provides safe covert for bird and beast and plant' and '[e]cologists investigate growth patterns and problems of erosion, and re-seed denuded slopes'. The work of Man to repair the work of Man. In 1991, the Nature

Conservancy Council evolved into Scottish Natural Heritage and is now NatureScot. In 2003, the Cairngorms National Park was established, encompassing not just the mountains but the area around across 4,500 square kilometres, making it the biggest in the UK. The longer I live here and the deeper I go into its beauty, the more I learn how precious this landscape is. The diversity of habitats – from the arctic tundra of the plateau to the Caledonian forests, to the marshes of the Spey – are home to an exceptional range of plants and creatures, many of them rare and at risk. A quarter of all the UK's endangered species are found here, and half the park's land is designated of international importance for nature.

But none of its land is owned or managed by the park authority. This responsibility lies with over fifty large-scale landowners and thousands of homes and businesses, an arrangement mirrored across all the national parks in the UK. In fact, the laws governing land use inside our parks are exactly the same as those outside of them. Across the nation, we have Special Areas of Conservation, Special Protection Areas and Sites of Special Scientific Interest and so on, but their regulations have nothing to do with park boundaries. This is quite different to my experience of national parks in Australia and South Asia, and I learned the issue lies with the name. The International Union for Conservation of Nature (IUCN), established in 1948, has an agreed system of categories for protected land based on management goals. According to that system, national parks are category two, whereas all the UK's 15 'national parks' are, in fact, category five, what the IUCN calls 'protected landscapes'. They have considerably lower requirements for ecological protection and a greater emphasis on the human and cultural heritage of an area.

The tale of how and why the UK applied the category two label to category five areas is not for this book, but it goes a long way to explaining why the Cairngorms, in spite of – and because of – their national park designation, remain a landscape of significant tension.

Another explanation is the issue of ownership. It is the second thing that struck me in my early hill walks in Scotland, after the more obvious blight of deforestation. I cheerfully assumed that if we were walking across land, it must be public. When my buddies explained that most of what I could see was held privately, I was astonished. While it was reassuring to discover that Scotland's liberal access laws meant we were not trespassing, the truth was still sobering. Scotland has one of the most unequal land ownership patterns in Europe, with large expanses owned by a small number of people. As detailed in Andy Wightman's book *The Poor Had No Lawyers*, such a distribution has arisen principally because of historic illegal or unethical actions and is retained by an opaque registration system and the political influence of the rich and powerful. Fortunately, thanks to significant campaigns in recent years, law and practice is changing.

There are many books devoted to these issues, so I will not expound them further except to reflect on their implications for the Cairngorms. The land of the park is owned by a mix of people and organisations: charities, such as the Royal Society for the Protection of Birds and the National Trust for Scotland; public bodies, such as NatureScot and Scottish Forestry; and private individuals, such as the King, whose Balmoral Estate sits in the south-east. Another is the Danish billionaire Anders Hoch Povlsen, who has overtaken the Duke of Buccleuch as Scotland's biggest private landowner. His holdings in the park include Glen Feshie, where I'm walking today and which I described in chapter six as a site of impressive regeneration. Clearly, wealth and possession can be put to good use. Very little land here, however, is under community ownership or management. The role of the National Park Authority, then, is to co-ordinate the work of the landowners, the five local authorities, businesses and other organisations towards meeting the park's four aims. Broadly, these aims include conservation of both natural and cultural heritage, promoting public access and enjoyment, sustainable use of natural resources and economic and social development. It seems obvious to me that these embody inherent conflicts, and the park seems to be caught in a purgatorial game of Twister in attempting to fulfil them all.

The questions at the heart of land ownership, use and regulation, is what the land is ultimately for and who gets to decide. Nan Shepherd's view of the mountain seems to be that it is not 'for' anything other than to exist in the fullness of its own life. She does not deny the human need to inhabit and utilise land but expresses a deeper human need to allow the land to inhabit us. Her respect for the mountain people she met arose partly from this. Of old James Downie, the Deeside farmer, she wrote, '[T]he stern grandeur of the corries had invaded his soul.' When Big Mary, her hostess at Whitewell, was unwilling to leave the spartan hill farm, even in old age, Shepherd observed how 'the long sweep of moor held her in spite of herself'. Of another old crofting woman, she said, 'In her youth she ran on the mountains and something of their wildness is still in her speech.'

* * *

As we move deeper into the corrie, sensing its spirit fill us, the slopes of grass and scree rise into cliffs, riven with shadows and forming a dramatic, spiky outline against the sky, quite unlike the smooth granite boulders more typical of the Cairngorms. About halfway up, hidden behind several twists and folds in the mountain, we come to the waterfall. Though

I love all the forms water can take – springs, rivers, lakes, marshes, oceans – I think falls are my favourite. Sometimes they occur where great rivers tip off plateaus, or in shifts in a landscape, but because they need height and drop to exist, they appear most often in mountains.

Coursing their way down the Himalayas of my childhood, waterfalls were seams of silver, carrying all the purity and cold of the high snows, catching the light and arcing it back in rainbows, thundering onto rocks. And they are wondrous places to swim. When our family lived in the village at the foot of the Annapurnas, a beloved Sunday walk was to a waterfall around the side of a nearby ridge. We spent happy hours there, playing in the water, picnicking on the sunny rocks and having family devotions in our outdoor chapel; all the while, the Lasti Shon stream plummeted down through dark cliffs that were shaggy with mosses and dripping ferns, fanning spray into the sunlight and landing with a roar in the glittering, green pool. I remember it as I reach the Coire Garbhlach fall, and in my sweaty breathlessness, I cannot resist. With clothes on the grass, I wobble over the hard stones and into water, so cold 'a sting of life is in its touch'. The fall is at the back of a steep cutting, and the deeper I go between the rock walls, the louder the sound, till all else is drummed out. Bracing, I drop down to my neck and, with a few strokes, arrive at the churning froth at the back. Big breath and a dive under; the force of the water pounds on my head till I come up gasping, my whole body beaten to life.

Drying in the sun at the edge, we watch the spray of water leaving the pool and on down the rocks. Like Shepherd, I could sit for ages 'gazing tranced at the running of water and listening to its song'. She said it was one of the experiences that brought her into a deep sense of clarity and presence. At any given moment, there is always the same volume of water flowing down, over the same arrangement of rocks and forming the same basic pattern of flow. Yet every moment is different. Each shower of droplets fans out in a slightly different pattern; each gurgling spill pulls and tugs in a different way; each second throws up a different kaleidoscope of light and colour, a different run of notes. There is repetition and constant surprise; physical laws and randomness. In the simple play of water over stone lies an ocean of mystery. It is this state of flux, of the world in constant flow and change, that the mystical tradition – and Shepherd – refers to as Becoming.

Birds unknown to me fly out from the upper side of the waterfall in a commotion of black and white wings. My gaze follows them from water to sky, and we gather ourselves. I wonder if water, like land, can be owned. And what of air? In many indigenous cultures, the idea that any landscape could belong to individuals is unthinkable. Instead, we belong to it.

Further up, the corrie unexpectedly widens to a valley carpeted with bog cotton, each white tuft a gauze of light. Looking back the way we've come, the folds of the mountain hide the route; looking forward, the cliffs form a curving rampart and it's hard to imagine a way out onto the plateau. Where narrow burns come down the slopes and cut across our trail, they are marked by mounds of soft, damp moss and clumps of harebells. This secret, sheltered place is a hammock of verdant growth and sweet air, and another invitation to pause and savour.

At the top of it, one massive boulder sits alone. It looks like a fist and seems a haunting and remote echo of the Black Lives Matter protests that have recently broken out across the world in response to the murder by Minneapolis police of George Floyd. Though there are many continental Europeans and a few people of African and Asian descent in our communities here, the strath is not very multi-cultural. After my upbringing, followed by university in the city of Melbourne, I have sorely missed that richness.

This idyllic stretch of the Highlands may seem far removed from the injustices of colonialism and the slave trade, but not so. Historians such as David Taylor and David Alston have highlighted the historic wealth and land purchase in the Speyside area from the proceeds of the East India Company and West Indies sugar plantations, in particular the compensation payments at the abolition of slavery. These payments were given, of course, to the former slave owners, not the slaves. Local people were also instrumental in the new colonies of the Antipodes and the Americas, where even those who had suffered the Clearances in Scotland went on to drive indigenous people from their lands, sometimes in brutal violence. As a white Australian, I know my own forebears were involved in the stealing of that country from the original peoples who had lived there for 60,000 years, who never presumed they owned it and never imagined anyone could, until it was too late. And I acknowledge my own participation in systems that continue to damage both people and land. I cannot claim to love the Earth and pretend otherwise.

The challenging fist of the boulder also makes me think of the Indian soldiers that were stationed at camps nearby during the Second World War. Several branches of the Royal Indian Army Service Corps, called Force K6, were in the UK assisting with animal transport and mountain warfare training. Some still in their teens, they came from the mountainous north-west of then India, now Pakistan, and worked alongside British and Allied forces preparing for Churchill's plot to invade Nazi-occupied Norway. The arctic weather conditions in the Cairngorms made them an ideal training ground, with several programmes underway in different locations, including Braemar, Rothiemurchus, Glenmore and Glen Feshie, often utilising Norwegian instructors. Some programmes were designed for elite commandos, like the Lovat Scouts, while others were for rank-and-file infantry.

In his book *The Cairngorms Scene and Unseen,* war veteran and mountain-lover Sydney Scroggie writes of his own gruelling experiences with the 52nd Lowland Division. 'Sweaty, jaded and melancholy, the representatives of this force stumbled about in the mists of Cairn Gorm and Bynack Mor, too exhausted to comprehend the military business at hand.' He describes the Indian soldiers as 'turbanned Sikhs and charcoal-complexioned Mahrattas who were wont in those crazy, mountain-warfare days to jingle on horseback through the remains of the old Caledonian timber with spur and pennon'd lance.' In fact, almost all the K6 who came to the Cairngorms were not Sikhs or Hindu Mahrattas, but Muslims; Scroggie was perhaps misled by the use of turbans in their uniform. Their riding skills, however, must have been legendary as they were recounted by that other great Cairngorms writer of the time, Seton Gordon. He met them 'on sequestered forest paths galloping furiously on horseback, crouching on their horses and balancing skilfully on the sharp bends, their black beards streaming in the wind. In appearance some of these Indian hillmen were not unlike the old type of Highland deer stalker, their bearing on foot was erect, they were tireless in walking, their keen eyes flashed.'

When I was a teenager in the mid 1980s in Pakistan, our family visited the northern area these men came from. Behind the farmers, shop keepers, bus drivers and householders going about their daily business, lay a backdrop of pervasive conflict. We stood on a dusty roadside outside Peshawar looking across an encampment of the Mujahideen, the displaced Afghans fighting for the freedom of their country from the Soviets. One branch is now called the Taliban. In the eastern foothills of the Safed Koh mountains, we visited the notorious Darra Adam Khel gun bazaar, centre of a largely unregulated munitions trade for over a hundred years, fuelled by the ongoing warfare of the region, from the tribal to the international. My dark-haired, heavy-browed brother might have passed for a Pathan, in flowing shalwar kameez and round felt hat, if not for his Nepali yak-wool jacket. In the dirt compound of a gun shop, he took up position behind a Russian heavy machine gun as the dealer squatted beside him, cheerfully detailing its active service in Afghanistan. The next day, in the packed train chugging up to the Khyber Pass, a man with a Kalashnikov over his shoulder and rounds of bullets across his chest came and stood by our seats. Like all the other people in the carriage, swaying together with the rocking of the train, he never took his eyes off us. My mother believes he was there for our protection. Such faith in the goodness of people, eclipsed only by her faith in the goodness of God, must have given her the blithe confidence to take her family where angels feared to tread.

Twenty-five years later, when I moved to this quiet strath in the Scottish Highlands, it seemed as remote as one could possibly get from the armoured men of Pakistan's mountains. I had never heard of Force K6, and it took a while to make the startling discovery that not only had they been here, but one of their camps was right on the shores of Loch Insh, where I walk several times a week. There were other camps spread across both the Speyside and Deeside flanks of the Cairngorms between June 1942 and October 1943, and together they numbered nearly 2,000 men, in many cases more than doubling the resident population. With their striking appearance, hundreds of pack mules, flocks of sheep for food, and tented sites – including field hospitals, mosques and mobile cinemas – they must have had an enormous impact on the community. By all accounts, they were popular, helping on farms, playing with local children, sharing their chapattis and stories from home. But – till 2022 – there was scant evidence of their presence, certainly in the upper Spey valley: no mention in a local museum, no photos on display, no panels or plaques. Memorials to the Norwegian and Canadian support during the war existed, but nothing about the Indians.

Intriguingly, Nan Shepherd didn't mention them, either. In fact, *The Living Mountain* makes only fleeting reference to the extensive military training that took place across these hills. In her chapter 'Man', she writes, 'Man's presence too is disturbingly evident, in these latter days, in the wrecked aeroplanes that lie scattered over the mountains. During the Second World War more planes (mostly training planes) crashed here than one cares to remember.' Erlend Clouston, executor of her estate, has suggested that wherever planes appear in her writing, including the fiction, they are a sign of man's failed experiment with progress. At the time, they had very little use outside a military context, and to Shepherd they represented the mechanisation that not only removed people from their connection with the land but enabled ever more devastating violence. She had a growing sense that people were being turned into cogs in a great and increasingly evil machine at the expense of our relationship not just with the natural world but with our own better selves. The plane wrecks were a sign to her of the failure and destructiveness of that machine.

But she doesn't mention the men. The planes would have come from distant air bases, but the soldiers were stationed all around the Cairngorms and were routinely struggling across the hills with packs, animals and artillery, in all weathers. Many readers of *The Living Mountain* have imagined that, with so many men away at war, the mountains were relatively unpeopled and Shepherd could roam them in splendid isolation. On some days, evidently, she did. But, in reality, the area was busier than ever, with nearly a dozen military camps fringing the range and frequent exercises involving hundreds of men and even more mules. In her 1977 foreword, the changes she notes include, 'Young soldiers learn the techniques of Adventure,' but not that they had also been there when she wrote the original, learning the techniques of War. It is particularly puzzling to me that she does not mention the Indian soldiers, as she was so drawn to Asian philosophies and the writings of Tagore.

At first, I wondered if, in writing *The Living Mountain,* Shepherd wanted to keep the Cairngorms her 'secret place of ease' and not speak of war. But on closer reading I noticed the references to the war planes and how '[i]n a moonless week, with overcast skies and wartime blackout, I walked night after night over the moory path from Whitewell to Upper Tullochgrue to hear the news broadcast'. She was not escapist. Her life had been invaded by both the world wars, and the 'Great War' was an important element in her extended short story *Descent from the Cross* and her second novel *The Weatherhouse.* But her notebook of quotations from that period includes these lines from Tao Te Ching: 'When armies are raised and the issues joined, it is he who does not delight in war who wins.' Perhaps in her Cairngorms writing, she touched on the background reality of war, but chose to deliberately turn away from it to train her body and mind instead on the ancient and elemental nature of the mountain. It's also possible she never encountered the Indian soldiers on the hill – it is a sprawling range – and perhaps she didn't know that the ones camped in the area were doing mountain training. For security reasons, such information was never in the media. On the other hand, locals always knew what was happening. I would imagine the Asian presence did interest her, but perhaps to her mind, it was so much a different story that it did not belong in *The Living Mountain*. We will never know.

What I do know is that when I was commissioned to write the text for The Cairngorm Story (the exhibition at the mountain ski base), the military training was discussed, but one of the team said, 'I'm sorry, but I don't like the war story.' It was not included. I do not like the war story, either, but I'm not so sure we can erase it. There is a danger that we create mountains – and, indeed, all 'nature' – in our own idealised image; a danger that we who are lucky enough to experience these as places of recreation or spiritual retreat choose not to recognise them also as home, or livelihood, or even hardship. Shepherd *did* acknowledge these other dimensions to the mountain's life, especially in her portrayal of the land workers that peopled the hills and provided hospitality to her, they who were at labour while she at leisure. She recognised that, for many of them, the mountains were work and not play, but added, 'I have not found it true, as many people maintain, that those who live beside the mountains do not love them.'

At the same time, she knew that the meaning of a mountain – as of anything – is profoundly shaped by subjective experience and perception. 'One has to look creatively to see this mass of rock as more than jag and pinnacle – as beauty. Else why did men for so many centuries think mountains repulsive?' That anyone did think that might be surprising to us today, but it was the dominant view for a long time, certainly in Europe. Mountains were places of fear and danger, of fierce animals, difficult passage, thugs and thieves, death, superstition, haunting and horror. It was only in the Romantic period of the late eighteenth and early nineteenth centuries that perceptions began to change. Even then, the sense of mountains as 'sublime' arose from the idea that they were a place of meeting God, which was still terrifying rather than soothing. One would fall on one's face in fear, not stretch out for a snooze. Gradually, the idea evolved that a mountain-top spiritual encounter could bring peace, enlightenment and personal upliftment, so, in turn, the word 'sublime' took on the connotations of beauty and heightened experience it carries today.

Changes in attitudes developed further when the aristocracy began to frequent mountains for sport. This was initially hunting and pony trekking, then mountaineering and finally snow sports. Places of fear became places of adventure, challenge and courage, and ultimately, as humans confronted – and in some cases conquered – a demanding landscape, another route to personal, even spiritual, growth emerged. But, as Shepherd observed, it demands a shift in perception, a deliberate creative act. The material stuff of the mountain remains unchanged.

All the more intriguing to me is that she never reflects on the irony that at the very time the Cairngorms were for her a landscape of beauty and self-discovery, they were for others the treacherous practice ground for a military plot. It is possible for mountains to be both, as they were for Sydney Scroggie. He had been a passionate hill-goer from youth, so despite the misery of his training there, and the loss of one leg and his eyesight in active service in Italy, he returned to make hundreds of ascents in the Cairngorms and to write his own tribute to them. 'Each hill trip,' he said, 'brings a catharsis to those who have the insight fully to perceive the horrors of the world.'

I wonder how the Indian soldiers felt about the Cairngorms. Some of them worked from the Mountain and Snow Warfare School based in Glen Feshie, right on the other side of the river from Coire Garbhlach, where I am walking today, among waterfalls and wildflowers. Although the men were strong and resilient, the mountains of northern Pakistan are a far cry from the Cairngorms, and the soldiers were not equipped for the savage weather. During a long, two-day exercise in October 1942 called 'The Sphinx', 178 British and Indian men with 243 mules climbed from Loch Einich to the plateau, where they were stricken by bitterly cold winds, sleet, rain and blinding mist. They arrived in Glen Feshie at 9.30 the second evening, but one of the Indian men was no longer with them. There is no explanation for what happened or at what point they realised he was missing. The next day, a search party found his body on a bleak and wind-scoured slope of Carn Ban Mor. The subsequent enquiry determined that the men were not properly fed and their clothing inadequate.

The Norway invasion, called Operation Jupiter, was never executed, and after four years away from their families, the men of Force K6 – The Indian Contingent (as they were later called) – were finally allowed to go home. The bodies of thirteen of them remain buried in Scottish cemeteries, while another was cremated in Aberdeen; most died of illnesses, such as TB. Nine graves are in nearby Kingussie, carved in Arabic and English and set at a different angle to the others, facing north. As with all Islamic burials, the bodies are laid with the face turned towards Mecca. A local lady, Isobel Harling, whose brother lies in a war grave in Belgium, took it upon herself to tend their graves, planting flowers and laying wreaths for her 'Indian boys' for over seventy years. 'We're all Jock Tamson's bairns,' she would explain, quoting a Scottish saying that means we're all the same under the skin. She and other local people quietly remembered them at every Armistice Day, and in 2018, for the first time, an official military ceremony including both army padre and imam was held to honour these soldiers. At last, in 2022, exactly eighty years after their first arrival in the strath, a memorial to Force K6 – The Indian Contingent RIASC – was erected in Kingussie.

Khan Muhammad, thirty-two, from Rawalpindi, son of Fakhar Din and Jan Begum, husband of Mirza Jan, lies here beside his brothers, looking not just to Mecca and the rising sun, but to the mountain on which he died.

XI.

SLEEP

*No one knows the mountain completely
who has not slept on it.*

For Shepherd, whether alone or in company, the important thing was to deepen the bond with the mountain. 'The presence of another person does not detract . . .' she said, 'if the other is the right sort of hill companion.' By this, she meant someone who was a kindred spirit with the place in the same way as her, and with whom conversation was illuminated by that depth of relationship. This did not require the person to have great experience or extent of 'knowledge' in the academic sense, but simply the receptivity of senses and mind that allowed identities to merge. To become one with the mountain. And so she enjoyed much of her Cairngorms exploring with others: guides, friends, students and children.

But for the fullness of her own union, she needed sometimes to go alone, to relinquish all other distractions and expose herself to unmediated, elemental encounter. So much of her writing demonstrates the acute focus born of this solitary engagement. We find intensity and clarity, a power in description that proves not only her gift with words but also the keen attention that underlay it, the alertness of her 'naked touch with experience'. It was an approach that arose from deliberate intention and practice. 'I can teach my body many skills by which to learn the nature of the mountain.' Much of the time, this was the training of the senses to be 'keyed' rather than dull, and the opening of the mind to see beyond ingrained readings of the world to the surprises of reality. And through this discipline she found the experience that transcends conscious observation and bypasses interpretation to attain direct connection, the experience she called 'quiescence'. It was sleep.

Describing the moments of drifting off while lying on the hill, she said, '[T]he mind grows limpid; the body melts; perception alone remains.' She camped out on the plateau often, soaking in the almost endless light of midsummer nights and finally sliding into 'deep and tranquil sleep'. But some of her most rewarding experiences were daytime snoozes – unsurprising considering how often she set off at dawn, which in high summer would be at least four a.m. The falling asleep was not the only delicious pleasure, but also the moment after waking, when her mind was empty and she felt nothing more than a body pressed against the mountain. 'At no other moment am I sunk quite so deeply into its life. I have let go my self.'

It sounded an experience to be sought. I had slept in the Cairngorms, camping with Alistair, but never by myself. And I had never done a long walk alone, either. Never just me and the mountain. I knew that to inhabit something of what Shepherd described, I would need to do both – and I wanted to, for myself, not just this book. But it was daunting. So much of following Nan Shepherd – as a woman, a walker and a writer – is. Such a trip seemed to hold all my inadequacies and anxieties in one weighty prospect and, in a deep, buried sump of my psyche, lay the fear that I couldn't do it.

I have a long history with fear. When I was young it was very specific: fear of the dark. Not even the dark itself, but of evil within the darkness. Like many children, I was afraid of something lurking under my bed and would take a running jump into it at night, preventing that hand snaking out and grabbing my ankle. But there was always the fear that the hand would slide up the side of the bed and grab me anyway. Or that the nameless beast from behind the door would pace quietly towards me. Those fears only really struck when I slept alone, which wasn't often. In the Nepali village, we all slept in one room, my parents on the floor and my brother and I in an ex-army canvas bunk bed. In many of the places we stayed as kids, Mark and I shared a bedroom, and, ironically, boarding school was helpful in that respect, too, as I always had room-mates. But when I did sleep alone, I could easily fall prey to fear. It wasn't all the time, and it wasn't always clear what triggered it, but whatever the origin, I didn't know what was worse: the lying awake feeling afraid or the nightmares.

The fear and the bad dreams always centred on the supernatural: demons, ghosts, witches, evil spirits. I only ever watched one horror film, aged thirteen, with a group of friends at the dilapidated Picture Palace in the Indian hill station of Mussoorie, and was haunted by it for years. Similarly, I've only read one horror book, around the same age. Or, half a horror book, to be precise, because my mother found it under my pillow and promptly threw it in the bin, muttering that my dreams were already bad enough. Of course, I protested, but she was right. Of course.

The struggle with fear continued till, at eighteen, having finished school and in Australia, I had to haul my mattress through to the floor of my brother's bedroom again. I decided this needed healing. My mother came with me for prayer from the pastor and wife of the big Baptist church I attended at the time. They were charismatic and caring, and prayed with quiet passion for my deliverance. There was no exorcism and I didn't start speaking in tongues, as they had hoped, but I have never again been overpowered by fear.

But nor have I done long walking or camping trips by myself. I started to wonder why. It's not avoidance of solitude, because I treasure it, both in the focused work of writing, but also in daily short walks and the occasional solo writing retreat. I don't think I was consciously avoiding it, but I had never actually felt the urge or even thought about it much before discovering Shepherd. There had always been enthusiastic company to hand – perfect hill companions – which I enjoyed. Perhaps, also, there was a residual notion from my South Asian upbringing that women do not go on outdoor expeditions alone, and if they do, they are asking for trouble. I don't agree with the principle, but when I was growing up in the seventies and eighties, few national women had opportunities or support for such adventures – for a range of social, cultural and economic reasons – and it probably influenced my expectations.

Partly because of that, the fears gradually shifted focus from spiritual attack to sexual. Like so many young women in India and Pakistan, I was regularly harassed and groped and sometimes followed, despite dressing in culturally appropriate ways and nearly always going in company. (It never happened to me in Nepal.) The situation was exacerbated by the widespread perception that white women were loose and fair game. It's one of the reasons I rarely went anywhere alone. Then, as a student in inner-city Melbourne with housemates doing gender studies and criminology, I became well acquainted with what went on in the 'west', too. So, the growing awareness of that threat added new strands to the rope of fear. But it was not so much personal anxiety as realism. Sometimes it makes sense to be afraid. A certain kind of fear is basic awareness and essential for navigating the world. You need to know what you're up against and how you will survive. Fear only becomes a problem when it hijacks your imagination and prevents you from embracing life. But despite my wariness – my *awareness*, if you will – I don't remember it cramping my choices as a student. In fact, I believed it should do no such thing: a woman is not to blame for sexual assault and should not be obliged to curtail her freedom to be safe from it. At the same time, I knew that the more vulnerable and exposed I was, the more likely I was to be attacked. Both are true. Ultimately, though, I avoided dark, lonely streets and solo outdoor adventures less from fear and more because I felt no need or desire for them. I did travel the world by myself at twenty-two, but rarely alone for long because I was always meeting up with others. Like Alistair. My perfect companion.

So now, all these years later and living on the hem of these mountains, why hadn't I camped out alone? Was it fear? Deep down, I think yes. A mixed-up bundle of fears: Could I manage all the practicalities like pitching the tent and lighting the fiddly stove by myself? Could I find the way? My navigational skills are 'emerging', at best, so would I get lost? Could I carry everything over a long walk without feeling too burdened to enjoy it? What if the weather turned foul and I was miserable? What if I fell and no one was around to help? I honestly felt the risk of physical attack up in the mountains was incredibly low, but still . . . what if some nasty or unstable person . . .? Most dominant of all, could I lie there alone all night in the dark and not feel afraid? What if fear settled over me again, as it had done so many times in my youth, and I was powerless to fight it? What then? Was I courting disaster?

Certainly, when I detailed my plans to my parents on the phone, my mother squawked, 'What are you doing *that* for?' Which is ironic, coming from a woman who let us ride on the roof of buses haring around mountain passes in Nepal and raised us in a remote village where there was no road, electricity or phone and with the aid only of a well-thumbed copy of *Where There Is No Doctor*. Perhaps she has softened in her old age.

I wonder what fears Shepherd faced in her solo Cairngorms walking. She speaks of the universal mountain goer's grappling with risk and danger, but says it hit her more in retrospect than at the time. 'Often, in my bed at home, I have remembered the places I have run lightly over with no sense of fear, and have gone cold to think of them. It seems to me then that I could never go back; my fear unmans me, horror is in my mouth. Yet when I go back, the same leap of the spirit carries me up.' In her near-death moment in Loch Avon, fear 'became a rare exhilaration' that enlarged her. She held a respectful fear for the forces of weather and water on the mountain and, knowing the scorn of the hill people for irresponsible walkers, she probably became increasingly conscientious in her timing and preparations. But she wasn't at first. 'Prudence – I had only once before been on a Cairngorm – told me to wait . . . But I couldn't wait. The morning was cloudless and blue, it was June, I was young. Nothing could have held me back.' That walk saw her suddenly 'swallowed up' by cloud and unable to see a thing. Perhaps it tempered future recklessness, but it did not scare her off. In 'Poem IV' from *In the Cairngorms*, she describes the view from Sgòran Dubh Mòr into Loch Einich in a snow storm:

> No man so sure of self but here he must tremble.
> Here man escapes from the futile sense of safety.

But she never mentions fear of the dark, or of assault, or of malevolent spirits or even the multitude anxieties that can beset the mind when alone.

For me, all those many fears existed, but it's not until writing them down now that they have gained a clarity they didn't have at the time of my planning. A bit like Shepherd only confronting her fears in retrospect. It's as if my pen is now a hook down into my subconscious which has just lifted a mass of dark stuff out of the pit for me to dissect and inspect. And that is the two-edged thing about fear. Sometimes we need to expose it and sometimes we need to ignore it. I definitely needed to tackle the tangible issues. Ignoring essential safety provisions *is* courting disaster and is unfair on loved ones and rescue services. So, I kept checking the Mountain Weather Information Service, knowing that as summer disappeared into autumn my opportunities for safe passage alone were dwindling. I waited for clear conditions, and I chose a straightforward, popular route with clear paths or very easy navigation. I practised putting up the tent and got Alistair to check my route plan and kit, packing plenty of warm and waterproof gear, first aid and chocolate.

But as for all the other fears, I just didn't give them oxygen. Ultimately, fear can become fear of fear itself and the more you give it air, the bigger it gets. But we all know that trying *not* to think about things has the opposite effect, so there's no use consciously suppressing fear either. The thing is to keep returning the mind to the good. My most important reason for heading out on a solo camp was not to conquer fear or prove something to myself or anyone else, but to embrace the mountains. To enter them fully, with nothing and no one separating us, and to entrust myself to night and darkness and sleep in the arms of the Maker.

* * *

I wanted to walk up Glen Einich to the long loch at the end because Shepherd wrote about it in her essay 'Wild Geese'. 'A gamekeeper told me once that on the night of every fifteenth of October, the migrating geese descend upon Loch Einach, filling its great hollow with the rushing of their wings. Here are their sleeping quarters as they pause on their journey from the north-west. That is the night, and I must go; he had been there, had seen them coming in their hundreds.' Though she never managed to go on that date, she wrote, 'I have spent in Glen Einach a whole October day that was punctuated by their harsh alien crying . . .'

For me, it is late September, but with a rare weather window, I decide to seize the chance. The only flaw in the forecast is high winds from the north of up to forty miles per hour on the Saturday afternoon and night. These winds would blow straight down the Einich valley, where I would be battling to erect my tent alone, but I figure it is still more sheltered than up on the plateau and worth the effort. When I set off, it is eleven degrees and the cool breeze is pushing dark clouds across a sky that fleetingly opens to sunshine and small scraps of blue. The forest and moor of Rothiemurchus are intensely quiet apart from the ringing of gun shots, possibly for grouse or for the clay pigeon range in the valley. I pass a group of young backpacking women setting up under a giant, spreading tree, as well as several walkers and mountain bikers, heading back down the valley. Stopping to talk with one family, we end up in a long and cheerful conversation about hillwalking, camp food and the merits of adding whisky to the morning porridge. After that, I am alone.

The inner needles of the Scots pine trees are turning yellow and further up, the bog asphodel, cross-leaved heath and grasses are all drying out to a papery copper. The broome and gorse have long since lost their flowers, and the black seed pods rattle as I swish past. The low-growing cowberries still carry some of their delicate white flowers along with clumps of bright red berries. Gradually, the trees thin out and disappear and as far as you can see up the glen and the slopes either side, there are none. The walk takes three hours up a steadily rising trail, and the sun has just disappeared behind Sgòr Gaoith ridge at seven p.m. when I arrive at the mouth of the loch. The opposite ridge, rising to Braeriach, is still glowing. There is no one else beside the loch and no geese on its rippling surface, scraped back against the current by the wind. Fighting the buffeting and the stony ground, I get the tent up, clearing my first hurdle, with no great speed or style, but sufficient to hold together. In the shelter of its southern side, I give thanks for the small miracle of stove, flame and water, all working together like a dream to brew my tea, and then with mug and chocolate biscuit in hand, I explore the shore. Shepherd spoke of 'the great southern rampart of Loch Einich'. It is the bottom curve of a long, narrow horseshoe of cliffs threaded with waterfalls that plunge down from the plateau above, their water today blowing back upwards in strong gusts. The crags bottom out into sloping banks of scree, grown over with old brown heather and patches of grass that lead down to the water.

Either side of the mouth of the loch, where the river runs shallow over the stones, there are two humps, overgrown with heather and moss. Closer inspection reveals blocky stone structures under the foliage which are all that remains of the old sluice gates here. They were once key infrastructure in the timber trade of the late eighteenth and early nineteenth centuries, where forestry men released water from the dammed loch, creating a torrent powerful enough to scoop up felled logs that had been laid downstream. Guided by river-side woodsmen, these logs bumped on down to the Spey where men called 'timmer floaters' lashed them into rafts and rode them to the coast. By that point in history, upper Glen Einich was already treeless, but the old Gaelic place names and ancient remains indicate it was once forest. Shepherd writes, '[B]y the sluice gates at the exit of Loch Einich, can be seen, half-sunk in the bog, numbers of the roots of trees long perished.' Those white wraiths are still there, in some cases thousands of years old, their pale limbs reaching out from the peat in silent witness. It's like a poster for a horror film that I could never watch.

By quarter past seven, all colour has drained from the glen, and the sky is clouding over in washes of grey, a soft white mist roiling down from the plateau. Darkness gradually slips like ink through the air, absorbing everything but the orange torch of Mars suspended above the southern ridge. I eat my dinner and wash up, and then it seems there is nothing left in this place but feeling and sound. Nothing but the hard ground and the wind flapping the tent, the water trickling over stones and the occasional croak of grouse. Lying in my bag, the wind becomes sinister, like something is approaching: the swish of fur through grass, the squelch of footsteps; it sounds like animals, then people, a brushing against the flaps, trailing hands, breath. Then there are distant horses galloping, something tearing, now ripping, now slashed. My tent is not far from the spot a young man was found dead in a blizzard a hundred years ago, but, thankfully, I only learn this later. I lie there and listen, my imagination wild with possibility, but my mind holding to a prayer for peace, a trust in the Presence.

It is a terrible night. Guarding against the cold, I put on all my clothes and wedge myself into the sleeping bag like stuffing in a chicken, then feel so trussed up and sticky I wriggle back out and shed some layers. But the rest of the night I am too cold – or is it just the air above me? Or the windward side of the tent that keeps whipping its icy breath into my face? Certainly, its noise rattles at me all night, the soundtrack of my waking and my weird dreams, so it becomes hard to distinguish. Despite my blow-up mat, the ground feels relentlessly hard and cold, and I toss and turn to get comfortable, only getting less so as I tangle my sleeping bag and rip the liner, feeling fettered as a captive.

But the main problem is my incredibly sore hips. It only occurs when I'm sleeping on the ground and it frustrates me, as I grew up being able to sleep anywhere – the floors of Indian railway stations, plastic chairs in airports, the back seats of heaving buses, top and tail on a narrow bunk with my brother. (Anywhere that I was not alone with my fears, of course.) My father, even into his eighties, is legendary for being able to stretch out and nod off on any surface with nothing more than a laptop for pillow and the possible luxury of a newspaper spread out beneath him. I know I'm simply suffering the inevitable signs of age, but I'm not as old as Dad and I don't want to lose the family gift. The gnawing ache in my hip joints and lower back keep waking me, till I finally rummage in the first aid kit and pop some painkillers. They kill no pain. It feels like any sleep is routed by wind, cold and aching, and I wake constantly in battle with them all.

I am reminded of Nan Shepherd's mountain snoozing: 'One neither thinks, nor desires, nor remembers, but dwells in pure intimacy with the tangible world.' No, of course I'm not bitter. In fairness, I don't think she was talking about nights in a battered tent. She knew what wind could do. In an essay titled 'Noises in the Night', she said, 'Ghost stories may conceivably be the monstrous progeny of this union of Night and Wind.' But the physical trials of my night really don't matter, in the end, because through it all, the one thing that *does* matter comes to pass: I am shielded from fear. Undoubtedly, it lurked out there in the dark, at unchartered borders of my mind and the buried vaults of memory, but it did not gain entry. I was tired, sore and grumpy, but I was not afraid.

And at some point in that afflicted night, I heard geese.

* * *

By six a.m., the wind has died away and there is a hint of light through the tent. I climb out into a bowl of stillness. The sky to the north-east is beginning to glow, its transclucent blue reflected in the looping bends of the river. Above the black cliffs, Mars has moved round to the west, and opposite him, the Morning Star shines like a beacon above the Braeriach ridge. Orion draws his bow across the southern sky, his three-studded belt my favourite constellation, as it is easily recognisable to me in all the places I have called home in Asia, Australia and Scotland. There are no clouds apart from a few small drifts low in the north. Without even a breeze, everything is so quiet I can now hear the distant plashing of the waterfalls. As the morning sunlight gradually steals down Sgòr Gaoith ridge and my eyes can take in more, I see twelve Canada geese floating in silence on the loch. Somewhere, on the flank of the hill, a songbird.

I begin my walk up onto the plateau by taking a direct route across the rough ground, but this proves fiendishly difficult to navigate. Comprised of tussocky mounds rising out of bog, it is so thick with foliage it's hard to tell which is which, and I stumble, teeter and plunge my way. It's particularly unstable with a heavy pack, so I'm relieved to join the path that rises diagonally out of Glen Einich and up to the Braeriach plateau. This is the one probably taken by the Sphinx training exercise in 1942 when Indian soldier, Khan Muhammad, died. That was 15 October, but instead of hundreds of geese, there were hundreds of soldiers, struggling up the narrow trail in atrocious conditions.

Here, at the end of September, many of the rocks are already frozen over and slippery, especially in the burns where verglas forms – that treacherous, invisible skin of ice over the stones. As I gain height, I look back at the light pouring down the cliffs opposite and throwing their coppery reflection into the loch. 'And in a long line of crags . . .' Shepherd observed, about the Loch Einich cliffs, 'each buttress is picked out like Vandyke lace.'

I arrive up onto the plateau into the span of the sun and the far-flung views. On all sides there are layers and layers of hills in soft blues, browns and mauves, smudged by mist, but still rendering each silhouette in distinct outline against the pale sky. There is not a hush of wind. Further up, at the first cairn, I can see north to a great ocean of smoky blue above the Dava Moor and Moray Firth. Even here the stillness is so absolute it feels like a presence. Nothing moves or speaks. I hear the faintest ringing, like cicadas, but don't know if it is a sound beyond me or just in my head. In Shepherd's poem 'On a Still Morning', these words:

> So if I bend my ear
> To silence, I grow aware
> The stir of sounds I have almost heard
> That are not quite there.

Snow, she observed, 'hardly ever fails to powder the plateau about the third week of September'. This is no longer always the case, but this year we had our first dusting two days ago and the ground up here is still flecked with it, bringing a dappling of colours: the wheat tones of the dried grass, the grey rocks and the white snow. Climbing higher towards the summit, I move into more snow, mainly caught on the northern side of the tufts of deer grass. Most of our wind blows up from the south-west, so a north wind is unusual

and cold, and when this one swept down on Friday, we felt
winter in its breath. At the top of each snowy clump, shards
of rime ice are frozen into delicate horizontal stacks, pointing
north; sometimes thin stalks of grass bear preposterously
large plumes of ice, studding the slope with intricate white
fans, all sparkling in the sun. As Shepherd noted, 'For once,
even the wind has been fixed.' Any rocks are also flanked
with snow and ice creations on the windward side, but the
warming stone has melted a gap between itself and the ice
so that sometimes the formation stands erect by itself. As
the sun climbs higher and stronger in the still day, pieces of
ice fall with soft noises like the flap of a bird's wing. It is the
only sound.

At the top of Braeriach, there is a light breeze blowing up
from Deeside and I set up my stove behind a rock, enjoying
hot tomato soup with my oatcakes. It is the second-highest
peak in the Cairngorms, but arguably has better views as it
is steeper on all sides than Ben Macdui. Most dramatic is
the vista south above its sheer cliffs and corries. Shepherd
observed that 'one does not look upwards to spectacular
peaks but downwards from the peaks to spectacular chasms'.
The long ravine of the Lairig Ghru opens out into a glen
stretching to the lower Grampian ranges, the Dee running
like a seam of gold down its course. To the south-east, the
peaks of Cairn Toul and Angel's Peak curve around their
shared corrie, where the high pool of An Lochain Uaine is
nestled. Today, it is deep black and shiny as obsidian.

Unsurprisingly for a clear Sunday, there are several other
people coming and going on Braeriach. It was one of the
ways I reassured my mother. There are more men, as usual,
but also two women, both solo like me, both running, unlike
me. One is stork thin and wearing only shorts and a singlet.
Presumably she can't risk getting cold or losing time, so after
a quick snap on her phone, she lopes off. Although Shepherd

believed racing against others across the Cairngorms reduced the experience to a game, she also said, 'Yet what a race-course for these boys to choose! To know the hills, and their own bodies, well enough to dare the exploit is their real achievement.' Clearly, when she wrote, women weren't among the runners, but I think she would have been pleased to see these ones today. Women are claiming ever more ground and knowledge, both of the hills and their own capacity – physical, emotional and social – to 'dare the exploit'.

There has been much discussion about whether Shepherd was a feminist and whether her account in *The Living Mountain* presents a distinctly female experience of mountains. By placing these ideas together there is, of course, a potential contradiction in terms. To some feminists, the whole point of women's equal entitlement to outdoor adventure is that their experience is on a par with men's and not to be distinguished. They enjoy the same elements, want the same successes, and are equally capable of exceptional achievement. Granted, the majority of women have less muscle bulk, brute strength and short-term speed than the majority of men, but they compensate in a mountain environment by having, in general, greater flexibility and, in some cases, increased endurance.

Thus far, however, women's overall experience of mountains is still burdened by a long history of social expectation that continues to affect the psychological and physical landscape. And not just in South Asia. When the Ladies' Alpine Club was founded in 1907, and the Ladies Scottish Climbing Club the year after, it was in a context of not just limited opportunities but outright opposition. Writing in *British Mountaineering* in 1909, a certain C.E. Benson warned male climbers to 'keep a watchful eye on the ladies . . . for the woman who has once over-walked herself seems doomed to be more or less of an invalid for life.' Although some men were considerably more open-minded and supportive – notably the family members of the women's clubs – derisive attitudes prevailed for a long time. In his 1940 classic of alpine literature, *L'Amateur d'Abîmes,* French author Samivel wrote scornfully of the 'lonely crows . . . aping men', concluding, 'True women are too tender for the rigours of the mountains, and men will not accept that they should penetrate their domain.' In one staggering sentence, he epitomises both prejudice against women and a man's proprietorial attitude to demanding terrain. Clearly, what is most at threat here is not the female person but the male ego.

Intriguingly, though, Shepherd never comments on the issue. In fact, *The Living Mountain* seems refreshingly unencumbered by sexual politics. When she wrote it in the mid-forties, the use of 'man' for 'humankind' was so prevalent there is no surprise she employed it. But by the time the book was published in 1977, when feminism was an established movement and language use was changing, she saw no need to change her own. More significantly, at no point in the book does she relate any experience or express any view to suggest she had a gendered experience of the mountain. She clearly valued the guidance of the men who first led her into the Cairngorms and never suggests they scorned her aspirations. Her companions included men, women and children, and she draws no comparisons between them and states no preference. Old James Downie of Braemar, farmer, ghillie and 'one of the truest hill lovers I have known', congratulated her on her first Cairngorms ascent with a solemn handshake. He had been guiding women since the days they rode in on ponies in 'trailing skirts and many petticoats', but reserved his disgust for Gladstone, who got as far as the Pools of Dee from Braemar but wouldn't go the half mile further up to see into Speyside. When, as a very old man, Downie insisted on carrying Shepherd's bag to the bus, she 'remonstrated, but was treated as I suppose he treated his lady climbers long before'. When she learned he had died soon after, she understood the gesture as a farewell act of kindness.

More importantly, Shepherd never suggests that her increasingly slow, sensory and meditative exploration was in any way more feminine, or that a focus on summits was more masculine. To the contrary, she acknowledges her own original obsession with the peaks that saw her racing up the hills to get there. She began with 'the lust for a mountain top' and it was only through time and long-acquaintance that she 'began to discover the mountain in itself'.

As I have read other mountain books and listened to other mountain lovers, it seems clear that ambitious, goal-oriented climbing is not the preserve of men – why else would the women's clubs have been founded? – just as languid, contemplative meandering is not the preserve of women. Nor is either approach mutually exclusive, or, indeed, inherently superior. Quite often, passionate mountain-lovers embrace both in a seamless experience that is both about personal achievement 'to pit oneself against the mountain', as Shepherd put it, but also receiving everything else the mountain has to offer. Nor, I believe, did Shepherd imagine her way of writing about landscape and nature was in any way more female, or that women had an innate capacity to experience and reflect upon nature with greater sensitivity. She was not impressed by a book on mountain holidays written by a woman because she felt it lacked substance and depth. Furthermore, the fellow writer with whom she had greatest affinity in terms of ideas and expression, and the one who best understood her work, was Neil Gunn. Of his approval of *The Living Mountain,* Shepherd was not surprised because 'our minds met in just such experiences as I was striving to describe'. Similarly, responses to the book have not, to my observation, been characterised by gender. I know of many men, including hard-bitten mountaineers, who have found deep resonance with her work, but also women who have not. The incomparable and much-admired Myrtle Simpson, intrepid climber, skiing pioneer and adventurer, who has a Polar Medal, a Scottish Award for Excellence in Mountain Culture and half a dozen books to her name, and still walks the hills in her nineties, told me, 'I couldn't *stand* the book when it first came out. All that nonsense about "the raindrops made me twinkle". Honestly, I don't think she gets the hills at all.' Simpson, however, does enjoy her novels.

Was Shepherd an early feminist? Her very close friend, the partially sighted and half-deaf author Agnes Mure Mackenzie, was a suffragette, but Shepherd was not. Her singleness may have been choice but was also widespread at the time because of all the men lost in the wars. Certainly, she was increasingly unconventional in her thinking and in her departure from the established church, and she was quietly progressive, according to her close acquaintance. In a letter to Neil Gunn in 1930, she described her role at the Aberdeen Teachers' Training College as a 'heaven appointed task of trying to prevent a few of the students who pass through our institution from conforming altogether to the approved patterns'. But her fiction offers a complex portrait of women's experience in which characters can be fulfilled both by a university education and a mothering role, can be both deceived and awakened by romantic love, and where the bonds of close-knit, rural communities can be both nurturing and stifling. Her poetry also seems conflicted on the nature of womanhood, especially in relation to love, but 'Poem XII' hints at the inner power she finds:

Now she may re-create herself.
Now is the primal day.

Probably her most powerful statement about the independent agency of women, however, was her walking the Cairngorms – particularly alone, which was rare at the time – casting convention and her clothes to the wind, and being so captivated by the experience that she didn't even think about gender. Or if she did, she couldn't be bothered to mention it.

As I talked with the various men who also stopped at the top of Braeriach for lunch (the women were running too fast), I was thankful for Shepherd's example that spurred me to take this walk alone. But thankful, also, that I am not alone. Mountain-goers, like pilgrims the world over, are a fellowship. Whether we journey side-by-side, or meet in short encounters on the trail, or follow the steps of previous walkers through time, we go in company. Next to the enormity of a mountain, any differences between us fade.

* * *

I turn to home and the year turns deeper into autumn. 'October is the coloured month,' wrote Shepherd and here, in my corner of the Cairngorms, it is vividly true. But it is also the usher of darkness. As night draws closer around each day, the hours of light become more intense, the lowering sun pierces, the colours glow. I reach out to this season, longing for it to last but knowing it is already slipping away, that its potency is its transience, the unbearable radiance of its passing.

After the endless light of Highland summer and the gentle settling of September, October dusk falls at dinner time, charcoal soft and tugging me home to the smells of wood smoke in cold air. Night unfurls herself, taking ever more time and space, spreading brighter stars and bigger moons across her black beauty. There will be owls and firesides. There will be dark.

And at last, I realise – almost by surprise – that I am not afraid. I can walk alone for I am not alone. I can love the dark, for 'even the darkness is not dark to you . . . And when I awake, I am still with you.'

XII.

BEING

Slowly I have found my way in.

Nan Shepherd fell into the thrall of the Cairngorms in childhood, gazing at them from afar, but imagining her love would go unrequited. When she took that first, daring walk alone into their outer reaches as a young woman, it was not so much the consummation of the relationship as its commencement. 'So my journey into an experience began,' she said. What she found became far more than what she initially sought, and her final chapter crystallises that discovery. 'Here,' she begins, 'may be lived a life of the senses so pure, so untouched by any mode of apprehension but their own, that the body may be said to think.' A startling image, usurping the mind, it begs the question: What is the body thinking? What does it come to know? After all, to *know* the mountain was her desire.

I, too, walked into this range for the first time in my twenties, but from such a different childhood with such different mountains that, although our boots covered the same ground, our journeys were entirely different. We all bring to a place everything we have come from, everything we have known, everything we are. But what Shepherd learned – and I am learning through her – is 'the process of living' by which we peel back those layers in order to have ever more unfiltered encounter, what the mystic Underhill calls, 'the direct sensation of life having communion with life'.

Two years after my first visit there, I returned to Lochain Uaine, the 'green lochan' held like a vessel under the wing of Angel's Peak. This time, we scrambled up the stony north ridge to the top, and though it was midsummer, we still needed jackets, hats and gloves. Rising mist gradually conquered the plateau and we dropped down into cloud. Just above the lochan, we heard birdsong. 'Sit quietly for a while,' Shepherd counselled, 'in some of the loneliest and most desolate crannies of the mountain . . . and a single snow bunting will sing with incredible sweetness beside you.' This was one.

The lochan gradually appeared out of the mist, not green but grey. From a distance, its glassy surface held the surrounding slopes and the heavy sky. Up close, it revealed submerged rocks in muted granite pink, fringed with dark mosses. The mirror to the outer world became the window to the one within. The day was cold, the water not inviting, but to my own surprise, I peeled off and entered. Shepherd described the plunge: '[A]s one slips under – the catch in the breath, like a wave held back, the glow that releases one's entire cosmos, running to the ends of the body as the spent wave runs out upon the sand.' At that moment, I *knew* the loch in all its reality and I knew I was alive. Getting dressed again and heading on home, through reindeer and mountain willows, through midges and grim rain, I knew I, too, had 'walked out of myself and into the mountain'.

* * *

Each walk is different. Each time I go, even on familiar trails, if I open myself, then both I and the mountain are made new. 'I add to it each time,' Shepherd says, so that gradually the knowing deepens.

It's three degrees in Glen Feshie on a late November morning, the sky to the west blue and clear. Above us, to the east, the dark bulk of the Cairngorms is topped with snow and a loose mustering of clouds. The dove greys and whites give way to radiant fringes and allow a shaft of sun to penetrate and set a distant slope shining. We pass stands of bare birch trees, their parchment trunks rising through cascades of dusky purple twigs. Shepherd felt they were 'loveliest of all when naked'. As we take the route up the hill through natural Scots pine forest, the track is carpeted in red needles, and new growth rises ever higher up the bare slopes. Even in winter, there are signs of new life. About halfway, the sun bursts above the ridge line, shooing away the clouds and rinsing the world in light. The brown slopes are brushed with gold where the long grasses catch the rays, and just ahead, we can see the three deep creases of the gullies south-west of Carn Ban Mor, locally nick-named Tom, Dick and Harry. Behind us, the valleys of the Feshie and the Spey unfurl in a mosaic of river-run, forest and field. Our house lies tucked into those folds, the house I have lived in, now, for longer than anywhere else. This has become a familiar trail.

The first time I walked it was also a November, in 1993, when Alistair and I were newly engaged, and up here from the Central Belt for a weekend with friends. In a photo taken on this exact spot halfway up the hill, we are surrounded by snow, and I am wearing the same cotton tracky trousers of my first Cairngorms walk the year before, a pompom beanie and a hand-knit Nepali jumper. There is always something of Nepal with me. Not necessarily a tangible object, but always an inner thread that winds right round my heart and keeps tugging me back. Almost entirely closed to outsiders till the early 1950s, that small, land-locked nation at the roof of the world has become a magnet for millions of visitors. Many go for the mountains, many for the spiritual search, many discover something of both. The people of Nepal are profoundly religious, and most would find the notion of 'spiritual but not religious' incongruous. Their religious life is indivisible from the rest of life, woven through daily practice in food, festivals, clothes, worship, house decoration and rites of passage. Including pilgrimage.

Brought up in the birthplace of Buddhism, I have been fascinated by Shepherd's statement in the last paragraph of the last chapter of *The Living Mountain*: 'I believe I now understand in some small measure why the Buddhist goes on pilgrimage to a mountain.' Though there are many significant pilgrimage sites around the world for Buddhists, the most revered is Mount Kailas in Tibet, also sacred to Hindus and Jains. One route is through Nepal. In *To a Mountain in Tibet*, Colin Thubron's haunting account of his own journey there, he recounts the hopes and longings of the people on the way, of several faiths and none, like himself. When asked by his guide, 'Why are you doing this, travelling alone?' he cannot answer out loud. But on the page, he confesses, 'I am doing this on account of the dead.' Wrestling with mortality and the unresolved grief of losing his parents and sister, Thubron's trail is paved with sadness, not just because of their deaths, but also because of the pilgrims who succumb on the way and of the corpses cut up and laid out in the sky burials. His narrative is infused with loss and emptiness, with incomprehension – at both the customs of the faithful and at the passing away of those he loves. What can it possibly mean? What, ultimately, does it lead to? It was witnessing age, disease and death that first set Gautama Buddha on his search for enlightenment, concluding that suffering was the primary reality of existence. When Shepherd wrote *The Living Mountain*, she also had lost a parent and her only sibling, but she does not refer to them.

She does speak of death. She recognises that part of the life of the total mountain demands it. The plants have their cycles, the animals perish and people must die, too, some at a ripe old age, like her beloved James Downie and Big Mary, others from untimely and terrible accidents in the mountains. No one knows when or how, but we all know we will die, and what we believe about death will shape our life.

As I have been writing this book, we have all lived with the suffering, disease and death caused by Covid. Alistair is a doctor, living with these as daily companions, before and beyond pandemics, but in this time we have also lived with the terminal diagnosis and passing of his father, Brian. He and Alistair's mother came for two final weeks in the summer of 2020 and walked slowly with us in a wildflower meadow, ignoring stiff joints and spreading cancers to bend and admire and name. Sunny yellow buttercups, three-headed bird's-foot trefoil, hawksweed with its skirt of petals, breeze-tousled harebells and white dots of eyebright. One morning, with strength that surprised us all – none more than himself – Brian rowed us across the loch in a wooden boat. Though all things lost certainty, he held faith. Another day, they settled into camp chairs as I had a swim. A strong breeze rose, chopping over the loch, and both sky and water looked like scrap metal. Brian sat perfectly still, staring across the waves into the teeth of the wind.

* * *

Shepherd's final paragraph prompted me to explore its meaning with Buddhists of different traditions. Her second sentence reads, 'The journey is itself part of the technique by which the god is sought.' For a Buddhist, however, god is not sought. There is no over-arching divine being who is beginning and end, origin or purpose. In Tibetan Buddhism, deeply influenced by the older Bon religion and closely entwined with tantric Hinduism, there exists a pantheon of gods and goddesses, angels and demons, who must be appeased or warded off, or entreated for protection, luck and mercy, but these are as supports towards the greater goal, which is enlightenment – nirvana – salvation. And that salvation is not entry to the presence of God but absence of distinct identities – your own or any god's – in a merging into one-ness. Traditionally, for many Buddhists and Hindus, this salvation is attained through the gaining of positive karma, or merit, to progress further up the ladder of reincarnation until the ultimate release from the cycle of life, death and re-birth. In other Buddhist traditions, particularly newer understandings evolving in the west, the emphasis is different, such as the seeking of truth or the life of compassion. I sense that Shepherd's use of 'god' here is a metaphor for whatever the pilgrim's ultimate goal is, be that truth, salvation or the divine.

And what was her own goal? It changed. 'At first I was seeking only sensous gratification . . . I was not interested in the mountain for itself, but for its effect upon me.' That is where most of us begin, with a seeking after our own pleasure for our own sake. Whereas, she goes on, 'as I grew older and less self-sufficient, I began to discover the mountain in itself'. What she describes is the transition demanded by all the great spiritual traditions, to transcend the self in order to know the Other.

We pause below Coire Ruadh, where three burns leak

from the mountain's side and braid together into Allt Ruadh. This is a different Red Corrie to the one on Braeriach and is where the body of the Indian soldier, Khan Muhammad, was found. It's a bleak and scoured place, with steep slopes that face into the prevailing wind, and there are no trees or boulders for shelter. Today, there is nothing but a scattering of frozen snow in the moss and the sound of the burn. Muslims also go on pilgrimage. Most important is the Hajj to Mecca, one of the five pillars of Islam. On the first day there, pilgrims climb Mount Arafat, the Mountain of Mercy, to pray to Allah for the forgiveness of sins.

Our quiet remembrance is broken by a grouse exploding from the heather with a raucous gargle, and we move on. Going higher, the snow gradually whitens the ground, but not in a smooth sheet. The work of yesterday's wind has carved its surface in rippled patterns and changing textures, so that each boot-fall is like a print on hand-made paper. It looks like the translucent pages I once found in a cave on the Annapurna circuit. The dry, sandy hollow was completely empty but for hundreds of rectangular papers covered in Tibetan texts, the script beautiful to me, but impenetrable. The mountain, too, holds a script.

People of many faiths go on pilgrimage to mountains. Every year, over 150,000 Sikhs visit Hemkund Lake in the Indian Himal, bathing in the freezing waters in a prayer for purification. Sinai, Zion and the Mount of Olives are sacred to all three Abrahamic religions, with countless pilgrims beating a trail to their foot-worn slopes. And, increasingly, people without religious affiliation are going on pilgrimage, all over the world, the number growing every year. They are often described as having 'no faith' but a long walk, especially in mountains, demands it. The question is not whether you believe or not, but what you believe, and sometimes, as Shepherd discovered, the answers may only emerge on the journey itself. And they may emerge as further questions, as more beginnings rather than endings. 'One never quite knows the mountain.'

We step out of clear sunshine into a wall of cloud. It is not damp but an intangible white breath on all sides that allows us to see only what is immediately ahead and nothing beyond. It is like one that Shepherd encountered, also on these Feshie hills, that held 'no sensation whatever'. The sun burns a huge disc into the ethereal vapour, but does not break through. By the time we get to the top of the ridge, the mist has thinned to gossamer, and the vaulting canopy above is not yet visible, but somehow palpable. Pilgrimage, like every mountain walk, is a journey into the unknown. What the un-named fourteenth-century mystic called The Cloud of Unknowing. There are no guarantees, no formulas, no deal that can be struck with either earth or heaven. 'One walks among elementals,' says Shepherd, 'and elementals are not governable.'

Through the veil, the distant lines of Braeriach, Angel's Peak and Cairn Toul begin to appear and disappear, till the mist dissolves and we can see the whole sweeping plateau, lightly skimmed with snow. The curves and corries of the mountain are now crystal sharp, holding luminous shadows like fallen feathers of the great sky that wings above us in every shade of blue.

In Shepherd's journey, she learned to trust her body to read the text of the mountain till she knew it deeply. She was clear that her knowledge could only ever be partial because our senses are limited and unable to detect all the properties of the material world, yet they are more than sufficient to reveal its wonder, given time and attention. And sometimes the revelation becomes a kind of transfiguration. 'It is an experience that grows; undistinguished days add their part, and now and then, unpredictable and unforgettable, come the hours when heaven and earth fall away and one sees a new creation. The many details – a stroke here, a stroke there – come for a moment into perfect focus, and one can read at last the word that has been from the beginning.' It's like an echo of John's gospel. *In the beginning was the Word and the Word was with God and the Word was God . . . Through him all things were made.*

We stop at the cairn on the rounded summit of Carn Ban Mor and look across to the plateau on the other side of the Glen Einich chasm, the loch hidden deep inside it. Leaning against the reddish, snow-speckled rocks of the cairn, eating my sandwiches, I realise what is absent in walking the mountains of Scotland. In Nepal and India, just like here, many passes and hilltops are marked by something – sometimes a heap of stones – but they are nearly always accompanied by signs of faith: prayer flags, shrines, carved or painted scriptures, symbols and offerings. In Scotland, apart from the occasional plaque, there is rarely a sign of anything. What do the cairns themselves signify?

This entire range has now taken its name from the one hill – Cairn Gorm – which translates from the Gaelic as 'blue cairn'. Who built the first cairns and why? Of course, we do not know, though some are believed to be hundreds of years old. The act of piling stones on top of each other in such places goes back to pre-history and extends across most cultures that have access to liftable rocks. Though some cairns in Scotland are memorials to events, they usually serve as landmarks, indicating not just a summit but a waypoint, often made for practical purposes in this kingdom of clouds. Gamekeepers built them on ridges to show where a route fell beyond the sightline; coastal communities placed them where fishing boats could get their bearings; villagers erected them in the middle of trackless moors to help people find their way. Whatever the origin, they are a marker to the traveller that you have arrived at a point of significance. Orientation, pause, decision. Quite often, it signals a time to rest and eat, like today, as it provides shelter from the worst of the weather. But was it ever a place of prayer?

Some cairns are topped by crosses, but this is rare and controversial, as is the making of new cairns. While the old ones are accepted as part of an ancient cultural heritage, if people lug rocks around today to add to or create newer ones, they are often rebuked. To purists, cairns represent human interference with the natural landscape and are potentially misleading, with many walkers who have relied on them making navigational errors. Shepherd notes them, without judgement, as one of the many signs of Man on the mountain. 'His presence is in the cairns, marking the summits, marking the paths, marking the spot where a man has died, or where a river is born.' But never marking a meeting with the gods. Or perhaps simply not with any sign of it, beyond the stones themselves.

Why, in reference to pilgrimage to a mountain, did she speak of the Buddhist? Despite her evident interest, she made no claim to be one. But then, many Buddhists, including the Dalai Lama, insist one doesn't need to convert or identify to lead a good Buddhist life. Perhaps it was the philosophy in which she found the closest resonance with her ideas about the inter-connectedness of all things and her one-ness with the mountain. 'I am a manifestation of its total life, as is the starry saxifrage or the white-winged ptarmigan.' But such ideas are not unique to Buddhism and emerge in several branches of the Judeo-Christian tree from which she came. I wonder what Shepherd made of the early Celtic church, rooted in Ireland and blossoming in Scotland from the sixth century. Its practice and theology were steeped not just in physical experience but in the ordinary and everyday. Richly entwined with the natural world, the Celtic tradition celebrated the revelation of God in skies, waves and earth, pictured the Holy Spirit as a wild goose, and welcomed Christ in the stranger. It was distinct from the pagan world it increasingly supplanted, as it did not teach all things to be inherently divine, but rather recognised the spirit and work of a higher God in and through all things.

I sense, ultimately, the relevance of the Asian philosophies to Shepherd in *The Living Mountain* was the emphasis on the body, not just as a way of thinking, but as a path to spiritual growth. In her last chapter, as well as comparing her mountain walking with Buddhist pilgrimage, she likens its effect to 'the controlled breathing of the Yogi'. The body not only opens us to what is real in the material world, but also to spiritual truth that lies somehow both within and beyond it. 'To apprehend things,' she wrote to Neil Gunn, 'walking on a hill, seeing the light change, the mist, the dark, being aware, using the whole of one's body to instruct the spirit – yes that is the secret life one has and knows that others have.' And that truth, that hidden life, is Being. 'It is therefore when the body is keyed to its highest potential and controlled to a profound harmony deepening into something that resembles trance, that I discover most nearly what it is *to be*.'

We head north along the wide ridge, our boots crunching on the white sandpaper snow. From a distance, the mats of frosted grass look like a furry pelt on the mountain's back; up close, they metamorphose into a haul of treasure. Snow is clinging to every single blade, a fuzzy, bright coating, sometimes massed on one side, many times thicker than the grass itself; by some miracle of nature, it neither bends nor breaks the stalk, but holds it upright, in its original elegant curve. On some stems, the snow has melted and re-frozen as ice, creating a clear, glittering formation like a diamond necklace. There is enough beauty and science in one tuft of winter grass to hold you for a day, a lifetime, perhaps, and

I kneel down to observe and photograph. Kneeling. It is the right posture. Shepherd knew the importance of stillness and reverance, which some would call prayer.

Speaking of the moments when 'one can read at last the word that has been from the beginning', she says they come 'most of all after hours of steady walking, with the long rhythm of motion sustained until motion is felt, not merely known by the brain, as the "still centre" of being'. I get up from the magical grasses and walk on. Up here now, on the plateau, it is clear and spacious, neither steep nor windy, and we fall into a gentle stride. 'There,' wrote Underhill, 'the rhythm of your duration is one with the rhythm of the Universal Life. There your essential self exists.' This sense of motion leading to stillness reflects the balance of action and contemplation, of the outer life and the inner, the awakened and the 'quiescent'.

But most mountain walking is hard work. Shepherd herself called it 'toiling'. Quite often we feel battered by the weather, tired, stiff and blistered, hungry and thirsty, out of breath and in pain. What then, is the body instructing the spirit? *You are alive,* it says, *but not invincible. You are human. You are mortal.* 'It is a journey into Being,' she wrote, 'for as I penetrate more deeply into the mountain's life, I penetrate also into my own.' The pilgrimage, therefore, becomes as much a search for the self as for a god. Though neither selfish nor self-absorbed, Shepherd is profoundly interested in the self, for it is only through the self – through body, mind and will – that it is possible to know the mountain. Or God. Or anything. For something to be known, there must be a knower. Here she expresses a paradox: how the individual must forget the self in order to experience the world, yet can only do so through being fully and sensuously present in one's own being. 'Walking thus, hour after hour, the senses keyed, one walks the flesh transparent. But no metaphor, transparent, or light as air, is adequate. The body is not made negligible, but paramount. Flesh is not annihilated but fulfilled. One is not bodiless, but essential body.'

From here, the landscape is a span of rolling mounds and grand curves, from the whale-back summits to the shadow-pooling corries, all in a palette of brown, white and blue. To our right, only the tops of the Glen Einich cliffs on the opposite side are visible, plunging into the hidden chasm; a tendril of mist syphons up from its southern end to form a low quilt of cloud on the saddle. It follows the route of the path, where two months ago I walked alone, and nearly eighty years ago, the Sphinx unit hauled their mortars, mules and men. Khan Muhammad was still among them, walking hour after hour into shattering blizzard till his body could take no more. What is death? Something fundamental and material changes in the body. Something stops. But what Becomes of the self? What happens to Being?

The crags on this side rise in square-edged towers of stone that appear to be teetering precariously, like blocks piled up by a child. We arrive at the high point of Sgòr Gaoith – the Peak of the Wind – and it is not the wind that bowls us over, but the vision. The tight horseshoe of crags plunges down through flowing skirts of earth and scree to Loch Einich. Its waters are still and deep, an impossible sapphire blue.

'For an hour I am beyond desire,' Shepherd writes. To transcend desire – detachment – is a key tenet of Buddhism, but I think in this moment she is not expressing the denial of desire so much as its fulfilment. In the meditative pace of walking, in the meditative *peace* of walking, she needs nothing more. 'It is not ecstasy, that leap out of the self that makes man like a god. I am not out of myself, but in myself.' The word comes from the Greek *ec-stasis*, meaning to 'stand outside'. Here she seems to echo the contemplatives who speak of *enstasy* – to 'stand inside'. In *The Living Mountain*

Shepherd reaches a synthesis of both, the union of elemental and sometimes competing forces, in the world and within herself, and brings shape to them in much the same way as the 'strange and beautiful forms' arising from 'the struggle between frost and the force in running water'.

Hidden beneath the middle-class, Aberdeen respectability, the academic rigour and practical spinsterhood, there lurks an almost primal wildness. It is simultaneously flame of passion and luminous mysticism, both sensual and spiritual – the 'fury of being' that her character Jenny feels in *A Pass in the Grampians*. Woven through her writing – both the published and the correspondence – are the golden threads of an essential nature that is more than just rational and material, but nevertheless grounded, just as lightning flares from sky to earth. 'Storm in the air wakes the hidden fires – lightning, the electric flickers we call fire flauchts.' She sees the magical as well as the mundane. Even *in* the mundane, for nothing really is. 'If one could combine the two?' she wrote to Neil Gunn, 'irradiate the common? That should make something universal.'

Time and again in her writing, Shepherd achieves exactly that. *The Living Mountain* brims with moments when ordinary – even drab – objects are elevated. She describes how 'a sodden and shapeless' shrub, when caught in a stream becomes 'a tree hung with light . . . I think of the Silver Bough of Celtic mythology and marvel that an enchantment can be made from so small a matter.' But hers is not a magical realism or a neo-paganism. She did not imagine her sparkling branch was the work of literal spells. Although she joked that the charms of certain outdoor experiences could make anyone start believing in magic, she went on to say, 'I do not like glamourie.' It's an old Scots word from folklore for the illusions faeries cast to trick people into believing in things that are not there. Such 'witchery' is a deliberate deception of the senses. Shepherd rejected these superstitions as a false imposition between the self and the world. What fascinated her was the deep magic of what is true and real.

In the same way, she resists an animist reading of the landscape, insisting 'it would be merely fanciful to suppose that some spirit or emanation of the mountain had intention'. Instead, she recognises that in the very substance and stuff of the material world, there is wonder; in the everyday workings of nature lie miracle; in ordinary beings we find extraordinary life. And, though Shepherd's engagement with the mountain is rooted in empiricism and science, what these tools reveal is how powerless they are to master the full character and meaning of the universe. But rather than despising them for it, she welcomes them for the searchlight they cast upon the great dark, the extent of all there is yet to discover. 'The more one learns . . . the more the mystery deepens.'

Shepherd does not deplore fairy tales themselves, for she knows the importance of myth in understanding who we are. She wrote of 'the two great divisions of the Kingdom of Story . . . Both are necessary – both mystery and certitude.' She often expresses this through images of light on the one hand and earth on the other. Roderick Watson discusses these in his introductions to her works with his essay 'To Know Being: Substance and spirit in the work of Nan Shepherd'. But, he argues, although she explores their different qualities and dimensions – literally and metaphorically – ultimately, she celebrates their union. She does not suggest they are one and the same, but that both are fundamental to reality. 'I love a broom-stick and also a walking stick. I want the moon and the Pleiades and buttons to fasten my coat . . . Are the supreme moments of human experience, very strange or very simple? I think both. We classify, but there is no real dividing line. Fire is in every habitation.'

The magic that Shepherd did believe in was the power of language to capture and convey life. She admired it in Gunn's work. About his book *The Drinking Well,* she said, '[T]here is a magic of phrase – the kind of magic that obliterates itself, so that the words seem to vanish into the thing they have conjured up.' He applauded the same skill in her work. Of *The Quarry Wood,* he wrote, 'Your feel for character is so sure that you positively do sleight-of-hand with it. This is magical, illuminating.' The whole point, for both of them, was not a 'glamourie' that obscured the truth but rather the vanishing act of the writer – and their words – so that the reader enters direct experience.

The 1934 *Glasgow Herald* reviewer of her poetry collection *In the Cairngorms* recognised that her magic was in the fusing of opposites. 'In its strength, in its restrained intensity, there is more than a hint of the volcanic fires that were the precursors of the granite of the North East. If the ordered, systemitised accuracy of the North East can be effectively combined with the passion of the old fires, we may yet see evolving a type of literature that will stand by itself in its strength and vigour . . . we have had them in the lyrics of Nan Shepherd.' One of the great powers of her vision, captured in all her writing, is this capacity to reconcile, or at least hold together in dynamic tension, these apparently competing forces. Her work resists reduction to any manifesto – feminist, environmental, political, religious – for she knows that people and the world are far more complex than ideologies, that both are always in states of change – 'caught in the act of Becoming' – and that we will never come to the end of our understanding. For to even presume that we have, is ignorance. 'Knowing another is endless.' This does not defeat her quest for knowledge and insight, in all its forms, but only animates it. 'Mystery deepens knowledge.'

Opposite us, two burns appear from north and south

on the Braeriach plateau, turning to tip side by side down Coire Dhondail in twin dark gashes, each splitting into several narrow veins. They look like serpents' heads with forked tongues. Of water, Shepherd observed, 'It slips out of holes in the earth like the ancient snake.' There are many ancient snakes of myth and creation. The one coiled around the Tree of the Knowledge of Good and Evil said, *You will not die. You will become like god.* What did Shepherd mean when she spoke of man becoming 'like a god'? A clue lies in 'Poem VI' from *In the Cairngorms*, where she says that if the speaker could witness a certain mountain light 'That lights the world unto its ends / As God Himself were by', then she 'at last shall know / a god's experience'.

Published in 1934, the poems carry several references to God, heaven and the divine. But in *The Living Mountain*, begun ten years later, Shepherd speaks of creation but not Creator. And though she references the Buddhist journey as a seeking for the god, she does not define her own in those terms. When describing the 'men of character' of the mountain crofts, she says they are 'upright, though "the Birkie up yonder" comes near enough to the thought most of them hold of God'. She never tells us her own thoughts. But her silence says a great deal.

And what of death? In the face of her own, she wrote to a friend that she did not believe in an afterlife. To another, she said, 'I hope it is true for those who have had a lean life. For myself – this has been so good, so fulfilling.' Her conception is perhaps best captured through the character of Tommy in her extended short story *Descent from the Cross*. 'He had never imagined, never dreamed, so overmastering a sense of wonder. God, how he loved this life – loved it so much that leaving it ceased to matter; each moment so full, so rounded and complete that while he lived it he wanted nothing else . . . As for death – that wasn't worth considering. There might be something, or there might not. He didn't much mind, for already he had known a life that was eternal and indestructible.'

The end of *The Living Mountain* is a joyous shout to life. 'I am.' The resounding affirmation of existence and its significance. But this is not really Buddhist. The Buddha taught that the world is empty of self; the journey to enlightenment is one of relinquishing distinct personal identity in order to merge with the ultimate consciousness. In emphasising the importance of the individual and the here-and-now substance of her Being, Shepherd speaks from her Judeo-Christian roots. When she uses the term 'creation', it is not just a synonym for nature, but with an implicit sense of beginning and intention. Significantly, she describes human experience of the natural world as a work of making in response. 'It is, as with all creation, matter impregnated with mind: but the resultant issue is a living spirit, a glow in the consciousness . . . So, simply to look on anything, such as a mountain, with the love that penetrates to its essence, is to widen the domain of being in the vastness of non-being. Man has no other reason for his existence.' 'Non-being' is not the same as death, for it can invade life. 'Being' is not just life, either, but the life of wholeness. And more than just the whole life, it is fired by love. Rather than love being another form of 'witchery' making us blind or conjuring a mirage, it enables the clearest, most incisive perception that spears right to the truth – the essence – of the thing observed. 'Being', therefore, is not merely existing, but existing in love.

In her poem 'Real Presence', she follows a series of images about clarity – stars, pools, dawn, skies – by saying:

> To such a clearness love is come at last,
> Not disembodied, transubstantiate,
> But substance and its essence now are one;

And love informs, yet is the form create.
No false gods now, the images o'ercast,
We are love's body, or we are undone.

In our own afternoon of clear skies, we walk on to Sgòran Dubh Mòr – the Big Black Peak. A gully down the western flank of this hill is the one that so entranced Shepherd in her gazing from afar that it 'thirled' her for life to the Cairngorms. Looking south, back the way we've come, almost invisible wraiths of mist swift across the plateau and disappear down into Loch Einich, while further south, cloud billows low and bubbling over the cauldron span of the Moine Mhor – the Great Moss. To the north, Glen Einich opens to acres of empty moor, a lumpy, brown blanket, torn and patched with swatches of burned heather in a pattern hauntingly reminiscent of military camouflage.

It was on this ridgeline, after 'toiling' up from Loch an Eilein, that Shepherd got her first close view of the Cairngorms on that long-ago October day. 'There was the whole plateau, glittering white, within reach of my fingers, an immaculate vision, sun-struck, lifting against a sky of dazzling blue. I drank and drank. I have not yet done drinking that draught. From that hour I belonged to the Cairngorms.' By the end, we cannot know for sure what Shepherd believed about heaven and earth, faith and the unknown, death or God. But we do know she had believed in life and known love.

We turn back to the west to make our way down Meall Buidhe and Geal-charn, a spine of hills flowing back into Glen Feshie. They are all double-coloured, dusky brown on the southern flanks but pale with snow on the northern. Beyond them, the valleys of the Feshie and the Spey are bowls of sunshine, their patterns of forest, field and habitation lucent in yellows and greens. It is not just my house down there, now – my 'habitation' – it is my home. I, too, belong to the

Cairngorms. Further still, the humpy Monadhliaths merge into a range of humpy clouds that are so like the mountains it takes our binoculars to tell the difference. Descending, we look back up at the cold slopes, the strange, overlapping shapes of the ground cover, like lotus petals, marked out by blue shadow-lines in the snow.

Speaking of her experiences of revelation, Shepherd said, 'These moments come unpredictably, yet governed, it would seem, by a law whose working is dimly understood.' They cannot be controlled or coerced, but only received as a gift. They are the work of grace. Our own work is not to earn it but to open ourselves to accept it. And this is not a passive work, but as Shepherd learned, a training of the self – the whole body and mind and spirit – to be in tune, so that when the moment comes, we do not miss it. The flame that powers that work – the thing to be pursued with fervour, the road to knowledge – is love.

Dostoevsky spelled that deep magic in *The Brothers Karamazov*, through Father Zosima. 'Love all God's creation, the whole and every grain of sand in it. Love every leaf, every ray of God's light. Love the animals, love the plants, love everything. If you love everything, you will perceive the divine mystery in things. Once you perceive it, you will begin to comprehend it better every day. And you will come at last to love the whole world with an all-embracing love.'

Like Shepherd, 'I have been the instrument of my own discovering.' Like her, and countless others before and since, I have come to know and love the Cairngorms. But it is only just beginning. Turning home, the lowering sun sets the rocks of the cairns glowing in rust and copper and spins gold through the grass heads. A birch tree is lit by hidden fires. The voice from the burning bush. I am that I am.

To know Being, this is the final grace accorded from the mountain.

ACKNOWLEDGEMENTS

I am indebted to the many kind people who helped me with research, feedback and support in the writing of this book, those who, in the words of Nan Shepherd, 'have instructed me, and harboured me, and been my friends in my journey into the mountain'.

ON NAN SHEPHERD: Erlend Clouston, executor of Nan Shepherd's estate, for hospitality, sharing her library, information and photos; Neil Roger, for sharing photos, correspondence, Grant Roger's diary and enthusiasm; Charlotte Peacock, for her impressive biography, *Into the Mountain: A Life of Nan Shepherd* – an invaluable resource – and for sharing information and answering multiple questions; Dr Kerri Andrews, for sharing her compiled correspondence of Nan Shepherd ahead of publication; Leith Penney, for sharing memories and family correspondence; Professor Alison Lumsden and Paula Williams for helpful conversations and emails; Dr Roderick Watson for sending over his essays. Thanks also to the Nan Shepherd Archive at National Library of Scotland for assistance.

ON THE CAIRNGORMS, GEOLOGY, ECOLOGY & WILDLIFE: John Lyall, for unforgettable guiding and his depth of mountain experience; Neil Reid for advice, encouragement and the consummate Cairngorms reading list; Will Boyd-Wallis and Andrew Painting on ecological issues; Piers Voysey on Rothiemurchus forestry; Thomas MacDonell for the story of Glen Feshie; Duncan MacDonald, Dave Pierce, Suzi Duncan and the late Mark Denman for showing me the birds; Sheila Mackay for Gaelic pronunciation; David Howarth and Campbell Slimon on ticks and midges; Heather Reid on weather; Andy Emery on geology; Marina Dennis on crofting; Hamish Napier and the Storylands Sessions for Cairngorms music and stories; Myrtle Simpson for books, conversation and a towering example of how to be an adventurous woman; a host of good folk from the Cairngorms National Park Authority for my residency opportunity and ongoing interest; Mountaineering Scotland for courses, resources and community.

ON PHILOSOPHICAL AND RELIGIOUS QUESTIONS: Satyapada, Tiratna Buddhist Community, Highlands; Dr Stephen Johnson, ecotherapist and Western Buddhist; Khandu Lama Joseph on Tibetan Buddhism; Professor John Drane for historic church culture in Scotland; Professor Jane Shaw and Associate Professor Robyn Wrigley-Carr on mysticism and Evelyn Underhill; Craig Stangroom for shared contemplation, wide and deep.

ON COLONIAL HISTORY OF THE AREA: David Taylor and Sarah Hobbs

ON FORCE K6 – THE INDIAN CONTINGENT: Ghee Bowman, Gaynoll Craig, Hamish Johnston, John Padgett, Tom Ramage, Heather Lawrie Taylor and Saqib Razzaq of Colourful Heritage.

Deepest gratitude to these kind folks who read an entire draft and offered helpful feedback and encouragement: Alistair Appleby, Erlend Clouston, Juliet Dunlop-Fraser, Stephen Johnson, John Lyall, Shasha Rastogi, Neil Reid, Craig Stangroom, Ilona Turnbull and, particularly, Marlin Schoonmaker for the twenty pages of notes!

My thanks to the tremendous Cathryn Summerhayes, my agent; to the whole marvellous, hard-working crew at Polygon who make it all happen – I appreciate every single one of you; to Jamie Crawford for the idea and editorial input, and Edward Crossan, for skilled editing and steadfast support through the journey of this book.

Finally, love and life-long gratitude to my parents, Warren and Jessie, for raising me in mountains and with the faith to move them; to my soul friends for walking life's pilgrimage with me; to Sam and Luke, for bringing joy to the trail; and most of all to Alistair, for carrying the heaviest load and for being my perfect companion, up hill and down home. Thank you for bringing me to the Cairngorms.

I could not have walked this range or written this book without the countless others who have beaten the path before me, both as mountain-goers and writers. Many of them are listed in the bibliography, but many are unknown to me. I am blessed by their legacy. Most of all, my gratitude to Nan Shepherd, for taking me to the hidden fires.

The author and the publisher would also like to thank the following publishers and estates who have generously given permission to reproduce quotes from Nan Shepherd's writing within this book:

The Living Mountain, copyright © Nan Shepherd, 2008. Extracts from *The Living Mountain: A Celebration of the Cairngorm Mountains of Scotland* by Nan Shepherd reproduced with permission of Canongate Books Ltd. *The Quarry Wood*, copyright © Sheila M. Clouston, 1928. Extracts from *The Quarry Wood* by Nan Shepherd reproduced with permission of Canongate Books Ltd. *The Grampian Quartet*, copyright © Nan Shepherd, 2008. Extracts from *The Grampian Quartet: The Quarry Wood: The Weatherhouse: A Pass in the Grampians: The Living Mountain* by Nan Shepherd reproduced with permission of Canongate Books Ltd. *The Weatherhouse*, copyright ©

BIBLIOGRAPHY

Abbs, Annabel, *Windswept: Why Women Walk* (Two Roads, 2021)

Allen, John, *Cairngorm John: A Life in Mountain Rescue* (Sandstone Press, 2019)

Alter, Steve, *Becoming a Mountain: Himalayan Journeys in Search of the Sacred and the Sublime* (Arcade, 2014)

Andrews, Kerri (ed.) *The Correspondence of Nan Shepherd, 1920–1980* (Edinburgh University Press, 2023)

Andrews, Kerri, *Wanderers: A History of Women Walking* (Reaktion Books, 2020)

Barnard, Camilla (ed.), Carter, Claire (ed.), Dawe, Heather (ed.), Mort, Helen (ed.), *Waymaking: An Anthology of Women's Adventure Writing, Poetry and Art* (Vertebrate Press, 2018)

Barr, Donald and Barr, Brian, *The Spey: From Source to Sea* (Luath Press, 2009)

Baxter, Colin and Goodier, Rawdon, *The Cairngorms: The Nature of the Land* (Colin Baxter Photography, 1990)

Bowman, Ghee, *The Indian Contingent: The Forgotten Muslim Soldiers of Dunkirk* (The History Press, 2020)

British Geological Survey, *Cairngorms: A Landscape Fashioned by Geology* (Scottish Natural Heritage, 2006)

British Geological Survey, *Scotland: The Creation of its Natural Landscape* (Scottish Natural Heritage, 1999)

Brooks, Wilson & Koch-Osborne, *Cairngorms Walks* (Jarrold, 2005)

Brown, Hamish (ed), *Seton Gordon's Cairngorms: An Anthology* (Whittles, 2010)

Brown, Tony, *Cairngorms National Park Wildlife* (Ice Publishing, 2009)

Bullivant, Nic, *Cairngorm Ranger: An Insider's View of the Cairngorm Mountains* (Matador, 2018)

Cohu, Will, *Out of the Woods: The Armchair Guide to Trees* (Short Books, 2007)

Cooper, Adrian, *Sacred Mountains: Ancient Wisdom and Modern Meanings* (Floris Books, 1997)

Cross, Ernest, *Walks in the Cairngorms Near Aviemore* (Luath Press 1989)

Crumley, Jim, *A High and Lonely Place: Sanctuary and Plight of the Cairngorms* (Jonathan Cape,1991)

Crumley, Jim, *The Great Wood: The Ancient Forest Wood* (Birlinn, 2011)

Crumley, Jim, *The Heart of the Cairngorms* (Colin Baxter Photography, 1997)

Dennis, Roy, *The Birds of Badenoch & Strathspey* (Colin Baxter Photography, 1995)

Forsyth, Rev Dr William, *In the Shadow of Cairngorm: Chronicles of the United Parishes of Abernethy and Kincardine* (The Northern Counties Publishing Co, 1900; Bothan Publications, Lynwilg Press (Ed. John K. Campbell) supported by SNH, 1999,)

Glen, Ann, *The Cairngorm Gateway* (Scottish Cultural Press, 2002)

Gordon, Seton, *The Cairngorm Hills of Scotland* (Cassell & Co, 1926)

Gordon, Seton, *Highways and Byways in the Central Highlands* (Macmillan, 1949)

Grant, Elizabeth, *Memoirs of A Highland Lady* (Canongate, 2006)

Evans, Paul, *How to See Nature* (Batsford, 2018)

Hetherington, David, *Conservation of Mountain Woodland in the Cairngorms National Park*, from *British Wildlife*, August 2018

Hunter, James, *From the Low Tide of the Sea to the Highest Mountain Tops: Community Ownership of Land in the Highlands and Islands of Scotland* (The Islands Book Trust, 2012)

Hunter, James, *On the Other Side of Sorrow: Nature and People in the Scottish Highlands* (Birlinn, 2014)

Johnston, Hamish, *A Corner of Pakistan in Scotland: The Untold Story of Force K6* (Colourful Heritage, 2018)

Journal of the Ladies Alpine Club, 1975

Kempe, Nick (ed.) & Wrightham, Mark (ed), *Hostile Habitats: Scotland's Mountain Environment* (Scottish Mountaineering Trust, 2006)

Kempton, Chris, *Force K6 The Indian Contingent: RIASC Mule Companies in France & UK 1939–1944* (Chris Kempton, 2019)

Laird, Ronald, *Some Low Level Walks in Strathspey* (The Melven Press, 1986)

Lawrie, Brian, *Mountains and Rivers: Dee Valley Poems from Source to Sea* (Malfranteaux Concepts, 2015)

Loader, Catharine M., *Cairngorm Adventure at Glenmore Lodge: Scottish Centre of Outdoor Training* (William Brown, 1952)

McConnochie, Alex Inkson; Wayte, Bryn, *Strathspey* (Lewis Smith, 1902; Deeside Books, 2013)

Macfarlane, Robert, *Landmarks* (Penguin, 2015)

Mahood, Kim, *Position Doubtful: Mapping Landscapes and Memories* (Scribe, 2016)

Marshall, Meryl, *Glen Feshie: The History and Archaeology of a Highland Glen* (North of Scotland Archaeological Society, 2013)

Monbiot, George, *Feral: Rewilding the Land, Sea and Human Life* (Penguin, 2014)

Murray, W.H., *Mountaineering in Scotland & Undiscovered Scotland* (Diadem Books,1992)

Murray, W.H., *The Evidence of Things Not Seen: A Mountaineer's Tale* (Baton Wicks, London, 2002)

No rivalry but different: Glenmore & Rothiemurchus in the 20th Century (Forestry Commission Scotland, 2010)

Painting, Andrew, *Regeneration: The Rescue of a Wild Land* (Birlinn, 2021)

Palmer, Albert Wentworth, *The Mountain Trail and Its Message* (The Pilgrim Press, 1911)

Peacock, Charlotte, *Into the Mountain: A Life of Nan Shepherd* (Galileo, 2017)

Poucher, W.A., *A Camera in the Cairngorms* (Chapman & Hall, 1947)

Rattray, Ed, *Scottish Skiing:The Golden Years 1950–1990* (Matador, 2011)

Russell, Helen, *The Past Around Us: History of the Parish of Alvie & Insh* (Drumcluan Books, 1995)

Scroggie, Sydney, *The Cairngorms: Scene and Unseen* (Scottish Mountaineering Trust, 1989)

Shepherd, Nan, *The Quarry Wood* (Constable, 1928; Canongate, 1996)

Shepherd, Nan, *The Weatherhouse* (Constable, 1930; Canongate, 1996)

Shepherd, Nan, *A Pass in the Grampians* (Constable, 1933; Canongate, 1996)

Shepherd, Nan, *In the Cairngorms* (Moray Press, 1934; Galileo, 2018)

Shepherd, Nan, *The Living Mountain* (Abderdeen University Press, 1977; Canongate, 2011)

Shepherd, Nan; Peacock, Charlotte (ed), *Wild Geese: A Collection of Nan Shepherd's Writing* (Galileo, 2018)

Simpson, Myrtle, *Skisters: The Story of Scottish Skiing* (Landmark, 1982)

Smout, T.C. (ed.) & Lambert, R.A. (ed.), *Rothiemurchus: Nature and People on a Highland Estate 1500–2000* (Scottish Cultural Press, 1999)

Steven, Helen, *Rising to the Challenge: 100 Years of the Ladies Scottish Climbing Club* (Scottish Mountaineering Trust, 2010)

Taylor, Kenny, *The Glen with More: A Guide to Glenmore Forest Park* (Forestry Commission Scotland)

The Cairngorm Club Journals Online; https://cairngormclub.org.
uk/journals/

Thomson, Amanda, *A Scots Dictionary of Nature* (Saraband,
2018)

Thubron, Colin, *To a Mountain in Tibet* (Vintage, 2012)

Townsend, Chris, *A Year in the Life of the Cairngorms* (Frances
Lincoln Limited, 2011)

Underhill, Evelyn, *Practical Mysticism: A Little Book for Normal
People* (Original 1914, Aziloth Books, 2011)

Walton, Samantha, *The Living World: Nan Shepherd and
Environmental Thought* (Bloomsbury Academic, 2020)

Watson, Adam, *Essays on Lone Trips, Hill Craft and Other Hill
Topics* (Paragon Publishing, 2016)

Watson, Adam, *The Cairngorms: Scottish Mountaineering Club
District Guide*, Fifth edition (Scottish Mountaineering Trust,
1975)

Watson, Adam and Nethersole-Thompson, Desmond, *The
Cairngorms: Their Natural History and Scenery* (Collins 1974)

Watson, Roderick, '"To know Being." Substance and spirit in
the work of Nan Shepherd', *The History of Scottish Women's
Writing*, ed. by Douglas Gifford, Dorothy McMillan (Edinburgh
University Press, 1997)

Watson, Roderick, '"To Get Leave to Live." Patterns of Identity,
Freedom and Defeat in the Fiction of Nan Shepherd', *Studies in
Scottish Fiction: Twentieth Century*, ed. by Joachim Schwend,
Horst W. Drescher (Peter Lang, 1990)

Watson, Roderick, Introductions to *The Quarry Wood*, *The
Weatherhouse*, *A Pass in the Grampians* and *The Living
Mountain* in *The Grampian Quartet* (Canongate, 1996)

Webster, Paul & Helen, *40 Shorter Walks:Aviemore and the
Cairngorms* (Pocket Mountains, 2016)

Wightman, Andy, *The Poor Had No Lawyers: Who Owns
Scotland (And How They Got it)* (Birlinn, 2010)

Wilson, Scott, *Scotland's Native Woodlands:Results from the Native Woodland Survey of Scotland* (Forestry Commission Scotland, 2014)

Wright, Susan; Cairns, Peter and Underdown, Nick, *Scotland: A Rewilding Journey* (Scotland: The Big Picture, 2018)

Wrigley-Carr, Robyn, *Music of Eternity: Advent Meditations with Evelyn Underhill* (SPCK, 2021)

The Nan Shepherd Archive at the National Library of Scotland

For a list of informative websites, research papers and other artists and projects that have responded to the Cairngorms and Nan Shepherd's work, see www.merrynglover.com

The website also gives a list of background reading underlying my Cairngorms-set novel *Of Stone and Sky* (Polygon, 2021), most of which also informed this book.